Joe DeVivo

BANDS!

*Growing Up in the 50's as an Untalented Musician
in an Italian-American Town*

Joe DeVivo

New Horizons Publishing Company

© 2003 by Joe DeVivo

All rights reserved. No part of this book may be reproduced or transmitted in any form or means, electronic or mechanical, including photocopying, recording, or by any information storage and retrieval system, without permission in writing from the author.

Inquiries should be addressed to:
DeVivo Press
P.O. Box 783
Wilmette, IL 60091

Cover by Chris Posdal
Design by Kate DeVivo
Photography by the author

LIBRARY OF CONGRESS CATALOGING-IN-PUBLICATION DATA

DeVivo, Joseph
      Bands!: Growing Up in the 50's as an Untalented Musician in an Italian-American Town

1. Humor   2. Music   3. History - New Castle, Pennsylvania   4. Biography

Index

Library of Congress Control Number: 2003101064

First Edition

ISBN 1-884687-34-2

Printed in the United States of America   Joseph DeVivo - 1938-

10 9 8 7 6 5 4 3 2 1

My story begins with a butcher boy and a witch doctor

I have been told two stories that happened when I was a baby.

One was that when I was in the crib and heard anybody sing the Italian song *The Butcher Boy*, I would wave my tiny baby arms in time to the music. Everybody was amazed. I was obviously a prodigy and would become a famous musician when I grew up.

The second story was even more amazing.

My mother told me that I was a crybaby. Literally. I cried all the time, nonstop. Neighbors would hear me late at night and complain.

Since she had lost her first son due to a childhood sickness, she was really worried about me. She was so worried that, without telling my father, and in spite of the fact that she was a good Catholic, she summoned a witch doctor she heard about who happened to be traveling through town at that time.

The witch doctor came to our house. He took one look at me and said to my mother, "You've already lost one son, haven't you?" My mother, scared, nodded yes.

"Well," he said, "you're going to lose this one too unless we do something about it."

He then proceeded to draw crosses in blood (chicken?), on my baby belly and on my baby forehead, and also on several walls and doors all over the house. Then he said some prayers in a language she didn't understand. And then I stopped crying.

These two events explain everything. Obviously I was born with a great musical talent. But through divine intervention it was sacrificed in order to save my life.

Table of Contents

My Story Begins v
Dedication ix
1 My First Clarinet Teacher: Mike Prescaro 1
2 New Castle, Pennsylvania 5
3 Pianos are from Venus, Clarinets from Mars 13
4 Notes 17
5 *Pal-Yat-Chee* 21
6 Clarinet Teacher #2: Albert Colella 25
7 *La Famiglia* 29
8 A Short Story 35
9 Sounds of a Summer Night 39
10 The Gulbransen 45
11 My Last Clarinet Teacher: Alphonse DeVivo 51
12 The Friendly Natives 57
13 Why I Switched from Clarinet to Bassoon 63
14 My Buddy Jim 67
15 The Bassoon 71
16 The *Incomplete Method für die Holzblasinstrumente* ... 75
17 Vic Huff 79
18 My Bassoon Career Takes Off! 83
19 My Pittsburgh Bassoon Lessons 87
20 Ben Spiegel 91
21 Last Lesson in Pittsburgh 95
22 A Poem from the 60's by Me 99
23 Band is King 103
24 A Digression 107
25 The New Castle Symphony 113
26 The March Begins 117
27 Ne-Ca-Hi 121

28	Friday Night Football	125
29	The Star-Spangled Banner	131
30	Of Red Coats and Blue Coats	135
31	Feasting	141
32	Feast Food	147
33	Number 59	151
34	Fireworks!	155
35	The Follansbee Gig	161
36	The Peckhorn	165
37	My Short Life as a Professional Musician	169
38	Mr. Petrillo	173
39	The Musician's Suit	177
40	Santy Claus	181
41	Band of Anglos	187
42	The Night We Met *The 1812 Overture*	193
43	Conventional Wisdom	197
44	Jammin' in Philly	201
45	Marching to Different Drummers	205
46	Joe Hahn	209
47	Swimming Pools, Sausage and Woodwind Quintets	213
48	The Audition	217
49	The Age of Innocents	221
50	You Can Take the Boy Out of the Band, But…	225
51	My Most Glorious Musical Moment of All Time	235
52	The Button	241
	Acknowledgements	245
	About the Figurines	247
	Index	255

Dedication

Over the years, many big and boring books have been written about the world's great musicians. But very few words have been written in honor of the real heroes of music—the unsung, unheard, untalented not-so-greats like me.

If it weren't for us, there wouldn't be enough students to go around for the truly talented musicians to teach, which would reduce their incomes drastically and force them to give up music and get real jobs.

Opera companies and symphony orchestras would go broke if we wannabes didn't participate in their performances the only way left to us: buying tickets season after season. And if everybody had the talent to play jazz and rock, there'd be nobody left to dance; there'd be nobody out in the audience snapping their fingers and tapping their toes.

This book is dedicated to all of us who have spent endless hours practicing and taking lessons only to give lackluster performances that brought us little applause, few medals and zero scholarships.

It's for all of the clarinet players who were constantly challenged and beaten out for 1st, later the 2nd, and then finally, embarrassingly, the 3rd chair in the school band.

It's for the trumpet players who were asked to switch to tuba because the band needed somebody to play the tuba, even badly, and the trumpet section wouldn't miss them.

It's for those brave little boys and girls who keep going back to their music lessons and playing the same pieces over and over and over again because they just don't get it.

It's for the second-chair oboist who missed her last chance for glory by breaking her only good reed just before the concert on the night the first-chair oboist got sick.

It's for any piano player who ever forgot the first notes of a memorized piece just before a recital.

It's for all those pathetic souls who counted measure after measure of rests during a performance of Ravel's *Bolero,* and then came in one measure too soon.

It's for every woodwind player who ever squeaked, every string player who ever scratched, every drummer who missed a beat and every trumpet player who forgot to empty the spit valve before playing that long, single, solo note to begin the overture to *Rienzi.*

Because while it cannot be denied that there was little glory in our lack of accomplishment, the world should know that there was a great deal of joy in our trying.

1
MY FIRST CLARINET TEACHER: MIKE PRESCARO

My first clarinet teacher was Mike Prescaro who lived two houses away from us (and whose daughter, Geraldine, was my first love, although then, when I was 8, she was an old lady of 11 and didn't know I existed).

Mike was the premier clarinet teacher in town. He taught just about everybody who amounted to anything on clarinet, for instance my two cousins, Al Colella and Al DeVivo.

You'd think with those credentials I'd be grateful to have him as a teacher. But I hated to take lessons from him. First of all, I didn't like him. Although Mike was highly respected and well-liked by grown-ups, he was one of those men who never warmed up to kids. He never told me I was getting big. He never punched me on the shoulder and said,

The Joe Dee Dixie Band about 1930 at the Christopher Columbus Hall. From left to right, Harry Cubbertson, Marsh Miller, Johnny Hill, Fatty Orlando, Rudy (Egizzi) Eagan, Joe DeRobbio, Tommy Natale, Victor Gaspare, Enzo Restivo, Mike Prescaro, Nick Caiazza. Photo courtesy of Mrs. Enzo Restivo.

"Hey kid, how ya doin'." He never gave me the traditional quarter that older Italian guys often gave their friends' kids on holidays.

But that was nothing compared to my lessons. It was bad enough that he would chew gum and crack it in my ear while I was playing, which drove me crazy. But there was also the child abuse. Every time I'd hit a bad note—which

3

was often because I didn't practice lots—he'd pull my ear! He'd reach right over and give it a big jerk—ow!—every time I hit a clinker.

Between the gum and the jerks, I was a nervous wreck.

Somehow, I don't know how, I managed to communicate to my father that this wasn't working out and we ended the lessons.

Or that's what I thought at the time. It had never occurred to me until now that there's a pretty good chance it was Mike who stopped the lessons, not me.

2
NEW CASTLE, PENNSYLVANIA

When somebody names something as big as a town, you'd think they'd be so proud of the responsibility they'd use a little creativity—it's not every day you get to name a town. But, from the looks of it, people are more proud of where they've been than where they are. Maybe it makes a little sense that there are Moscows, Londons, Romes and Pragues all over the United States because they're names of world capitals. But New Castles? My computer's mapping program shows 26 of them sprinkled all over the country. That's not even counting the counties. Or the New Castles in other countries. (I have a picture of my wife standing in front of a sign in Italy that welcomes you to, you guessed it, Nuovocastello!)

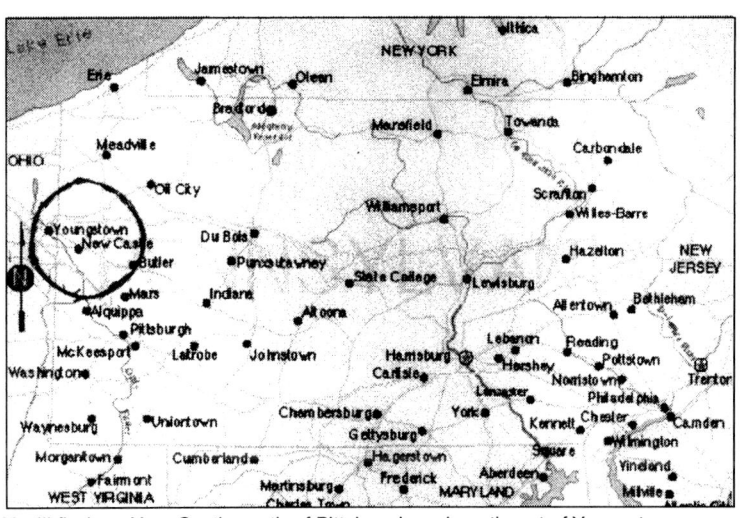
You'll find my New Castle north of Pittsburgh and southeast of Youngstown.

I had always assumed that New Castle, Pennsylvania was named after Newcastle, England. But John Carlysle Stewart, who laid out the town way back in 1798, named it after his home town, New Castle, Delaware. Since that New Castle in Delaware was named after Newcastle, England, we're talking here of a third-generation New Castle.

I never appreciated the hills of New Castle was until I moved away to live in the flatness of Illinois. Although I eventually learned to love the minimalist beauty of the big sky and straight-line horizon of the Midwest, to this day I miss the ups and downs of Western Pennsylvania.

You'll find New Castle 50 miles north of Pittsburgh and 20 miles east of Youngstown, Ohio. Many people know it as the first exit on the Pennsylvania Turnpike going east, or as the last exit going west.

Comfortably nestled in a valley with big hills and three rivers, New Castle has old iron bridges, large parks with waterfalls, and several grand mansions. Most people live in modest two- or three-bedroom homes that they decorate even when it's not a holiday. They put friendship candles in their windows, have vegetable gardens, their lawns are well-watered and neatly manicured, and you'll often see a Madonna blessing the yard. And like folks from the other New Castles all over the world, they are really tired of hearing jokes about hauling coals back to it.

About half the people in New Castle are of Italian descent, with most of their ancestors coming from the same part of Italy, the province of Caserta, a little northeast of Naples. The other half is made up of everything else. There are Jews, Syrians, Lebanese, Greeks, Poles, Blacks, Irish and even a bunch of White Anglo-Saxies. And there are also the black-suited Amish living just north of town, horse-and-buggying down Route 18, taking their eggs and cheese and hard labor into town to sell.

For all that diversity, people generally got along with each other. We went to the same high school, played in the same bands and ball teams, shopped in the same stores. We also went to each other's parties and picnics and ate each other's wonderful foods and danced to each other's music. We seemed to enjoy our differences more than most places.

I'm sure there was plenty of prejudice floating around, but most of it floated above my head or beyond my eyesight. Actually, the most blatant bigotry I witnessed as I was growing up was directed at Italians by other Italians. Everybody knew the *Bruzzese* (Italians from Abruzzi) were *capotost'* (hard heads), i.e., stubborn. And the *Calabrese* (Italians from Calabria) were known to be very crafty. I never found out what the Casertans were known for, but I doubt that the *Bruzzese* and *Calabrese* thought we were perfect.

New Castle has had its brushes with fame over the years. The Warner brothers opened their first movie house there. Shenango Pottery was the country's biggest maker of china and its logo can still be found under cups and plates all over the world, including several sets of White House china. A high school classmate of mine, Walter Mangham, held the United States high school record in the high jump for many years. Chuck Tanner was the manager of the Pittsburgh Pirates in '79 when they won the World Series (he now owns a popular restaurant in New Castle near my mother's old house). And many of the fireworks that exploded all over the country to welcome in the new millennium, and the ones that lit up the skies of New York City to celebrate the Statue of Liberty's last big birthday bash—they came from New Castle.

For me, New Castle was a town filled with music. Maybe for other boys, it was filled with baseball, or with hunting and fishing. But for an Italian-American kid with my particular set of family, neighbors, and holy days of obligation, it was music everyplace you turned. I woke up every single Sunday morning to the smell of spaghetti sauce and the sounds of my mother's favorite radio program of Italian music. I couldn't understand a word, but I can still hum a few bars of the theme song. Then it was high mass at St. Mary's where my father was the choir director. After I grew out of my altar-boyhood, my favorite place to sit through the boredom of mass was up in the choir loft. Not only was it close to the music, it was the best place to look down upon the worshipping congregation and check out every girl in church. But the best part was that it was easy to leave the moment you reached the part of the mass that constituted the least amount you had to sit through and not go to hell when you died. So right after communion, I was out of there—along with a lot of smokers who couldn't wait to light up.

During the rest of the week, since my youngest sister and I both took music lessons, our house on Mercer Street was filled with the sounds of me occasionally practicing clarinet and Janice constantly practicing piano. And almost every night after dinner, the two of us delayed our nightly chore of washing and drying the dishes by going to the piano where I would sing to her piano accompaniment. My *Vesti la Giubba* is a family legend that's still talked about. It was that bad.

By the time I got to be a teenager, in spite of my rocky start with Mike Prescaro, I was going to all kinds of band rehearsals and parades and concerts. I played in my schools' bands and orchestras; the New Castle American Legion band; the Salem, Ohio, American Legion Band; the Red Coat and the Blue Coat bands; and for a short time, the Greenville, Pennsylvania Symphony. And I was a member of the Youngstown University opera orchestra for their production of Mozart's *Magic Flute* even though I was still in high school at the time.

Once a week, I'd go with my buddy Kent Malley out to my sister Ev's house in the country where he, and some other pals of mine, took French horn lessons from her husband, Ken Meine. I was very envious of them. They played an instrument that could be heard in the balcony. At that time, I was playing bassoon. Not only was its sound on the subtle side, the old guys in the Italian bands laughed when I sat down to play. "Ay! Looka! Itsa farting bedapost."

There were the family parties where my father would play the mandolin and lead the kids in singing *The Green Grass Grows All Around.* And with his brother Tom on guitar they'd play and sing Italian songs, some of them with dirty words judging from the "ooh!'s" and behind-the-hand laughter of my mother and aunts. Uncle Tom knew how to chord, but didn't know when to play them without his brother's help. My father would softly tell him "do" or "sol" or another key for him to switch to when it was time to change chords.

There were my father's choir rehearsals and the men in the choir coming over to the house after mass on Christmas Day to toast the holiday with a shot of Seagram's 7 followed by an Iron City Beer chaser and Christmas carols around our piano.

There were all the pre-wedding serenades under the bedroom windows of brides-to-be by a pick-up group of musicians. And the weddings themselves with the blue-suited dance bands playing the latest hits, some standards, and of course tarantellas, polkas, mazurkas and for a big finish, the "cake march." There were my sister Janice's piano recitals. And my cousin Louie Colella's clarinet recitals. (I was never good enough to recite.) There was going to my Aunt Jenny's to listen to Paul Lavalle and the Band of America on radio, and listening at home to my cousin Al Colella's band on WKST playing a jazz version of the *William Tell Overture*. And there were Mario Lanza, Spike Jones, and Richard Strauss records to play on the Victrola. (By then, our record player wasn't a Victrola, but we still called it that, just like we called our GE refrigerator an ice box.) And every Saturday afternoon, my sister Anita listened to the live broadcasts from the Met during her weekly chore of cleaning the bathroom. And on Saturday night, while doing the dishes, Evelyn listened to Arturo Toscanini conducting the NBC Symphony, live from New York.

There were the sock hops, proms and dancing to the big bands at Cascade Park in town and at Idora Park over the border in Youngstown, Ohio. There were the Syrian picnics with their sexy line dancing and the Greek parties with their twirling handkerchief dance. And there were the many summer celebrations, or feast days, to honor various saints by eating, gambling, listening to band concerts and shooting off fireworks, occasionally all at the same time.

There was all the odd-moment humming, singing, whistling and dancing all over the place.

To tell you the truth, I don't know how anybody got anything done.

3
PIANOS ARE FROM VENUS, CLARINETS FROM MARS

All three of my sisters took piano lessons from a Mr. Thomas Morgan who came to the house once a week. My youngest sister Janice eventually switched to a Miss Virginia Woods who must have been a better teacher because Janice had to go to *her* house for the lessons. (To me, it sounded like she was going to camp once a week. I wanted to go to Virginia Woods, too, and sit by the campfire and tell ghost stories.)

In my family, the piano was for girls.

The clarinet was what the boys took up. So when I was 8 years old, my father bought me a used clarinet for $20. I was to follow in the footsteps of my clarinet-playing cousins Alphonse, Albert, and Louie.

At first, I was really jealous of my sisters being able play an instrument that they didn't have to assemble and wet a reed for. They could just sit down and play whenever the mood hit them. By the time I put my clarinet together and sucked on the reed until it was ready, I was usually out of the mood.

On the other hand, I don't know how pianists do it. How can they read so many notes? Clarinet players sometimes get notes that come in flurries and have to be played inhumanly fast. And each note, no matter how fast it's played, has to have its own pattern of finger placements. The fingers have to cover the holes completely, the tongue has be timed perfectly with the fingers, the mouth and lips have to be set just so, the air column has to be constantly adjusted, and you have to be very careful you don't breathe in the wrong places.

But, bottom line, a clarinetist has to read only one note at a time.

I don't see how anybody can read all the notes a pianist has to read, let alone play them.

It's just not possible. You want proof? See the next page.

Mathematical Proof!

To the right are the
last few bars
of a popular piano solo,
Rachmaninoff's
Prelude in D-flat.
Count the notes.

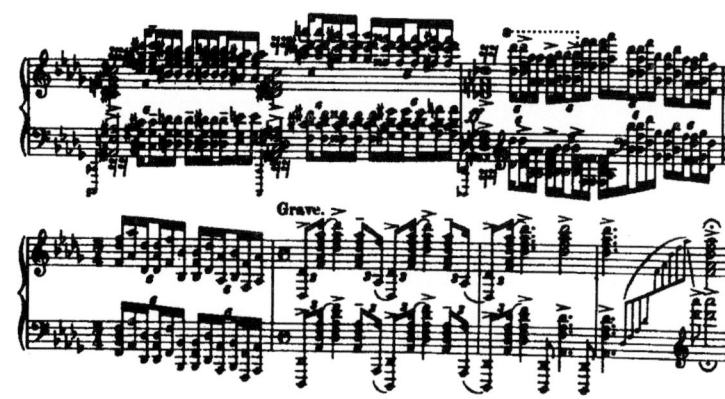

Here are the last few bars of
a popular clarinet solo,
Weber's *Concertino*.)
Count the notes.

I rest my case.

4
NOTES

Beginning piano students are lucky. On their very first lesson, when they hit a key and a note comes out, it sounds pretty close to what it would sound like if Bach, Bernstein or Brubeck had hit that very same note when they were at the top of their games.

But when a beginning clarinet player tries to play his first note, what he gets is a god-awful, fingernail-scraping-blackboard kind of sound. That's if he's lucky. If he isn't, he'll get an ear-piercing glass-shattering squeak that'll send dogs, cats and parents running for cover. It takes a long time for a clarinet student to develop a sound safe enough to play in public.

Those first lessons, whether for piano or clarinet, are boring. A kid goes into them expecting to learn songs and become the life of the party right away. But what you play instead of the latest hit tune are single notes, first for one beat, then for two, then for three, and finally for four beats. And when you have that mastered, you get to play another note, first for one beat, then for two, then for three and finally for four beats. After months of this, if you have shown that you have talent enough to continue, you graduate to scales and exercises. And finally, maybe after a year or so, if you've practiced and practiced and made good progress, you reach your goal. You get to play a real song. *Mary Had a Little Lamb.* Oh joy!

Back in 1884, a magazine called *Etude* was first published as "a monthly journal for the musician, the music student and all music lovers." For many years it was read by teachers and students who were dedicated to the art and elegance of music (as opposed to certain ear-pulling, gum-chewing neighbors I could mention). The artwork on the covers of *Etude* was always beautiful, and the magazine had a "nice" way of putting things. Here is a little beginning-student poem I recently found in an old issue:

NOTES

The first big note, without a stem
Is WHOLE NOTE, round and white.

And next in line, with long black stem,
Big HALF NOTE stands upright.

The QUARTER NOTE, with long stem, too,
As black as black can be,

While EIGHTH NOTE looks like quarter note,
But has a flag, you see.

What note is this? With two black flags?
SIXTEENTH beyond a doubt.

Your music book now take, my child
And try to pick them out.

5
PAL-YAT-CHEE

As I have mentioned (see Chapter 2), my rendition of *Vesti La Giubba* from the opera *Pagliacci* was a memorable one, especially the part where the clown cries. That was my best part since I didn't have to cry in tune. For some reason, no one ever recorded my version of the aria, so it's lost forever. But there's another special version that was recorded. It's probably out of print, but maybe you can find it on eBay. It's really worth looking for. It's called *Pal-Yat-Chee* and it's by Homer and Jethro.

If you start at the *Vesti la Giubba* part of the aria, take it about 50 times faster than Leoncavallo intended and use a countryfied twang, you can sing right along with them. Their tale of woe describes a show they accidently went to where a fat guy in a clown suit sang:

> Invest in a tuba and sumthin' or nother 'bout Cuba.
> He sung about a lady who weighed two hundred and eighty.
> When she takes a powder, he just starts chirpin' louder.
> And he won't do a gol dern thing 'cept to stand up there and sing.
>
> When we listen to Pal-Yat-Chee, we get all itchy and scratchy.
> This sure is top corn, so we go and buy some popcorn.
> We hate to go back, but we can't get our dough back.
> Ain't no use complainin' cuz outside it's a-rainin'.
>
> Seven hours later we're still in the durn theater,
> Takin turns a nappin', awaitin fer sumthin' to happen.
> Pal-Yat-Chee, he ain't hurryin, but the folks on stage are flurryin'
> And it sounds like Ketchy-tur-i-an's neighbor dance.
>
> Then Old Pal-Yat-Chee finds a guy,
> He's singin' cheek-to-cheek with his wife,

He grabs a knife and stabs the louse who stole his spouse,
And then he stabs himself.
T'aint very san-i-ta-ry.
They all collapse, but ol' Pal-Yat-Chee sets up, then he gets up,
Sings "I am dyin', I am dyin', I am dyin' "
We start cryin' cuz to tell the truth, we're dyin' too!

As the footlights fade out, we see Pal-Yat-Chee laid out.
But the dagger never caused it, Pal-Yat-Chee was plumb exhausted.

Reeeee-deeeeee Pagliocc-chioooooo. Soooo-form-a-(BURP)*

---

*Thanks to Ken Albin. I met him on eBay and he was nice enough to mail the words to me.

6
CLARINET TEACHER #2: ALBERT COLELLA

After my disastrous lessons with Mike, my father told me he was giving my clarinet away. But he hid it in his bedroom closet instead. He knew. After a couple of months, I begged him to let me take clarinet lessons again, promising to practice and practice until I had lips like iron and fingers that moved faster than the eye could see. So he brought out the old $20 clarinet again, and we went to cousin Albert Colella for lessons.

Al was a great clarinetist. After military service in World War II, he was invited to join the Army Band in Washington D.C., which was a cushy job and would have made him a hero among local musicians. And I'm sure he had other opportunities. But I guess he was too anchored to family, New Castle and a way of life to leave town.

He had played in an Army band during the war (as did Alphonse DeVivo. Music kept my family out of harm's way during the war). When he got discharged, he married a very pretty girl, Helen, and came home to become a pasta salesman. Later he owned a shoe store.

But his real profession was music. He taught the clarinet to countless kids, many of whom grew up to play and teach in the area. His dance band played for many weddings and proms, and it also played on his own weekly radio show on New Castle's WKST. He was an important member of the Saint Margaret's Blue Coat Band and eventually would become its conductor.

Like so many musicians in town, he would spend most summer weekends throughout the western Pennsylvania/eastern Ohio/northern West Virginia area at saints' day celebrations playing for parades, concerts and fireworks. And he also directed St. Lucy's church choir where my father and several cousins used to sing.

Al was the exact opposite of Mike Prescaro. He was soft-spoken and nice.

Going to his house for lessons was almost a religious experience. No, it was a religious experience. If I didn't have a good lesson, I felt like I had to go to confession. Like a good priest, Al was so understanding about my failures and so forgiving of my faults that I felt guilty every time I didn't practice enough, hit wrong notes or squeaked. ("Forgive me Father, for I have squeaked"?)

In spite of this, or maybe because of it, I learned a lot from Al. Or at least my fingers did.

All those damned scales and exercises were beginning to have some effect.

But finally it got to me. It hit me one day that I hated exercises and scales. I hated to practice and I hated my lessons. Yes, I had become a fairly good clarinet player with Al's help, but I couldn't take it anymore. I didn't want to take any more lessons. Ever again.

So somehow, again with a lot of help from my very understanding father, I found a way to gracefully stop taking lessons from Al. I'm sure Al didn't put up a fight, even a gentle one.

But, before I leave Al, we have to discuss my pet peeve about clarinet teachers. In every clarinet lesson I took, there came a point where my teacher wanted to show me how to play a certain passage by playing it himself. That was okay. Except before they played that passage they had to warm up on their own clarinet. Have you ever heard a good clarinet player warm up? It sounds wonderful! The fingers fly at ultrasonic speeds and notes fall in a beautiful torrent. There are scales, bits and pieces of melodies, themes, and riffs. And each one of those notes is perfectly formed, flung out and then followed with more. They'd go through about five minutes of this intimidating stuff, and then they'd ask me to play the passage again so they could show me how to do it right.

Every time this happened, I wanted to eat my reed and go home.

7
LA FAMIGLIA

I think I'd better help you separate the Alberts from the Alphonses and put the rest of my family in their proper places. What follows is a very brief description of my parents, siblings, and significant others. Feel free to refer to it any time you get confused.

According to family legend, my father, Joe DeVivo, fell in love with my mother, Helen DeMasi, when they were teenagers going to choir practice at St. Lucy's church. At that time, my father stuttered. And my mother had something called Bell's palsy which made her mouth look lopsided. Obviously, they were made for each other. To shorten a long and complicated story involving a school for stutterers in Indianapolis, the Depression, winemaking, lots of food and my grandmother's distrust of musicians—my father overcame his stuttering and my grandmother's objections, my mother's mouth straightened up, and they got married. And stayed that way for almost 70 years.

My father had come to this country from Italy in 1912 when he was 9 years old. He got a job with the B&O Railroad when he was 14 and worked for them for 50 years except during the Depression when he had to moonlight at odd jobs like selling Electrolux vacuum cleaners door-to-door and hanging wallpaper. But his life was the Church and music. He taught himself to play trumpet and other brass instruments. He played guitar and mandolin at parties and family gatherings. He sang in church choirs and eventually became the choir director at St. Mary's, the largest Catholic church in town.

My mother was born in this country, but she just made it. Her older siblings were born in Italy. She always had an impressive, hard-to-please intellect and I'm positive she had the ability to manage a giant corporation. But like most women of her time, she had to be satisfied with managing her husband, and becoming a terrific cook and mother.

I don't want to accuse my mother of joining the choir just to meet potential suitors, but once my mother got her man, she was never heard to sing again.

I have three sisters. The oldest is Evelyn who took piano lessons when she was a kid and was noted for her enthusiastic and rather percussive style of playing. She eventually followed her natural tendencies and switched to percussion instruments. When she was in her twenties and became the tympanist with the short-lived New Castle Symphony, she met and married a French horn player. They had four sons and wound up in Chicago. Before her retirement, Evelyn was the Manager of Special Services for the Chicago Symphony. Two of Evelyn's sons are in music: Glenn owns the Silver Moon, a blues bar in Wisconsin, and performs regularly with his own blues band. Curt, a conservationist in Wisconsin, like his grandfather plays guitar and mandolin at every opportunity. Evelyn's other two sons, Ken and Lee, though not performers, have connected with music over the years.

Anita, some years younger than Evelyn, also started out on piano but switched to oboe in high school. She was also a member of the New Castle Symphony and played in several wind groups. She got an English degree from Youngstown University, a Master's from Brandeis, and eventually became a highly-respected editor of journals, books and magazines in Washington D.C. She discovered choral singing there, became a founding member of the Choral Arts Society and even recorded a Haydn mass with Leonard Bernstein that won a Grammy. She's now back in New Castle, still editing, still singing, and occasionally, still playing the oboe.

Next came me. My mother decided to call me "Jody" instead of "Joey" because there were about a thousand other boys in town named after St. Joseph, or after fathers who were named after St. Joseph, and every single one of them was a "Joey."

Finally there came Janice, the baby of the family. She started with the piano and never switched to anything else. After high school she started her musical career, playing and conducting musicals at the Kenley Players in Warren, Ohio; then she did operas in Florida and toured with a Broadway company. After one marriage and two daughters, she got a Master's in conducting from Indiana University, and then did a lot of work in music education. She now lives in New York and in Europe where she plays and conducts musical theater productions. Her husband, David, an obsessive-compulsive but very accomplished guitarist, is often in the orchestras she conducts.

My father's sister, Jenny, and her husband, Louis Colella, had three sons. You already met Albert, my second clarinet teacher. Vito plays violin, string bass and percussion. And Louie, Jr., who was a just a few years older than me, conducts, plays and teaches clarinet at universities in the area. And he married a clarinetist. These cousins' kids have grown up to play, conduct and teach music throughout the area. Aunt Jennie and Uncle Louie also had a daughter, Mary, who, of course, took piano lessons (see chapter 3).

My father's brother, Tom DeVivo, and his wife, Aunt Lizzie, had a son, Alphonse, (who was also one of my clarinet teachers—you'll meet him later), and two daughters. Their daughter Barbara, has a son, Tommy Zumpella, who is a clarinetist, director of band music at New Castle High School and director of the Red Coat Band. And Barbara's sister Rose has one of the prettiest soprano voices in the family.

Another sister, Maria Bencivenga was a singer. She often performed with Aunt Jenny and Uncle Tom in musical dramas at the local playhouse in Mahoningtown.

My mother's side is a lot easier. The DeMasi family is full of many colorful and wonderful people, but for the most part, they can't carry a tune. (I'm pretty sure I got my musical ability from Mom's side.) She had four sisters and two brothers, but only Aunt Stella and her husband, Uncle Johnnie Lombardo, produced a musician— my cousin Ralphy.

Ralphy, a year younger than me, had one of those silver metal, indestructible clarinets that you could use as a weapon if you had to. While he never became one of the town's great clarinet players, he did become a good musician. And eventually, he found his main talent was acting and singing in musical comedies, which he did in theaters throughout the area.

Ralphy's a big guy, *really* big*, and has a big voice. He was born to play Nathan Detroit. Today he sings in a semi-pro choir in California.

If I drew a family tree, it would probably slightly lean towards my mother's side since they outnumber and outweigh my father's side. But if you suddenly took everybody away except the musicians, the tree would whip over and bend low on my father's side. There'd be only Ralphy on Mom's side, hanging on for dear life.

---

*When Ralphy graduated college, he decided to apply for the officers training program for the Naval Reserves. The only trouble was they had a weight requirement. No problem. Ralphy entered New Castle's St. Francis Hospital and starved himself for a week under a doctor's supervision. He lost about 30 pounds, managed to walk to the weigh-in under his own power, and made the weight requirement with a few ounces to spare. Immediately after the weigh-in, though, his friends had to help him to the nearest pizza parlor

8
A SHORT STORY

The Night My Clarinet Died

It happened while I was still taking lessons from Al Colella.

My clarinet was still the old $20 one my father bought for me. We had repadded the keys, so it was in playable shape. The case it came in, however, was another story. It couldn't be rehabilitated and soon crumbled out of existence.

Getting a new clarinet case took a while because in those days you didn't just go out and buy something when you needed it. You had to talk to a guy who knew somebody who could get it for you a little cheaper but it might take some time. So until we got a new one, I just kept the clarinet assembled.

There came a dark and gloomy night when my father was driving me home from a lesson. My caseless clarinet lay assembled and forgotten on the back seat of the Studebaker. When we turned onto Montgomery Avenue, my father stopped the car to offer a ride to two extremely heavy neighborhood ladies.

The End

9
SOUNDS OF A SUMMER NIGHT

In 1948, when I was 10 years old, we moved. We sold our side of the double house we shared with Uncle Tom and Aunt Lizzie in Mahoningtown, a suburb of New Castle that's about 99% Italian.

We became "Cake Eaters." Our new house was on Mercer Street on the city's North Hill. It was only about 25% Italian. Our new next door neighbors were the Appels, a middle-aged German couple.

Mrs. Appel was a warm, cheerful, large lady whose greatest asset was her friendship with the Figley family who lived a few blocks away. Their daughter, Judy, was in my new 4th grade class at Highland School, and unbelievably beautiful.

Mr. Appel, for all I know, was a sensitive, caring person but his heavy guttural accent and gruffness of manner led me to think otherwise.

The Appels had a dachshund named Waldy who has nothing do with this story, so you can forget about him.

The Appels and the DeVivos got along pretty well. My mother and Mrs. Appel enjoyed discovering the differences and similarities in their traditions and upbringing and, of course, trading recipes. My father and Mr. Appel borrowed tools from one another and while they didn't exactly develop a close friendship, they did occasionally knock back a backyard Iron City or two together. And when I mowed our lawn, I followed my father's directive and always mowed a little more than I had to between the houses. Sometimes, maybe because I thought news of my good deeds would get back to Judy Figley, I'd even mow their whole yard for free, without their asking.

It was a nice, neighborly relationship. Until "the incident."

Let me say right here and now that I don't blame Mr. Appel a bit. He had a right.

But I must also say that I was truly impressed with my mother. She stood up and protected me like a mother bear defending her cub against a mountain lion. I had never seen this in her before. Up until then, everything that went wrong was my fault. (Like the pancakes on the ceiling, for instance.) But this time, I was the victim! It felt great.

It happened on the eve of one of my clarinet lessons with Al Colella. (My clarinet had been repaired by now and I had a new case for it.) As usual, I hadn't practiced all week, so I had a lot to learn quickly. But on this particular night, due to one procrastination or another, I didn't start going over my lesson until after 9 p.m.

Once I started to practice, though, I went at it long and hard. I practiced scales over and over again. I practiced new fingerings on the high notes, over and over again. Sure, I squeaked, over and over again. Sure, the pitch of my high notes was gut-wrenchingly close, but not quite there, over and over again. But my lip, as I had promised my father, was like iron. I was going to play forever.

Did I happen to mention that this was a very hot summer night? And all our windows were open and so were the Appels' windows? And that Mr. Appel went to work around 5 a.m. so he was an early-to-bed person?

So it was no wonder that sometime after 10 p.m., I heard a loud, guttural, gruff voice screaming, "Shut dat goddam kid up zo peeble can get zome zleep around here!"

I froze. Was he yelling at me? Suddenly, I realized that my practicing was not as private as I thought. Then I looked at the time. Oops. Obviously, Mr. Appel's request was a reasonable one. So I put my clarinet away.

My mother, on the other hand, went ballistic. She had been getting some fresh air on our front porch and had heard Mr. Appel loud and clear. She didn't care about reasonable requests. Or even about the fact that my playing was also driving her nuts. There was no way that anybody was going to get away with calling any of her children a "goddam kid." Our house was filled with "Who the hell does he think he is!" and "The nerve!" and "He'll practice any damn time he wants!" and I'm sure she said some worse things, but most of what she said was in Italian so I didn't understand it all. She yelled out the window at the Appels' house. She yelled at my father. She yelled at to whom it may concern.

But she never yelled at me.

Many folks in the neighborhood got to sleep a little later than usual that night.

And things were never quite the same between us and the Appels after that.

10
THE GULBRANSEN

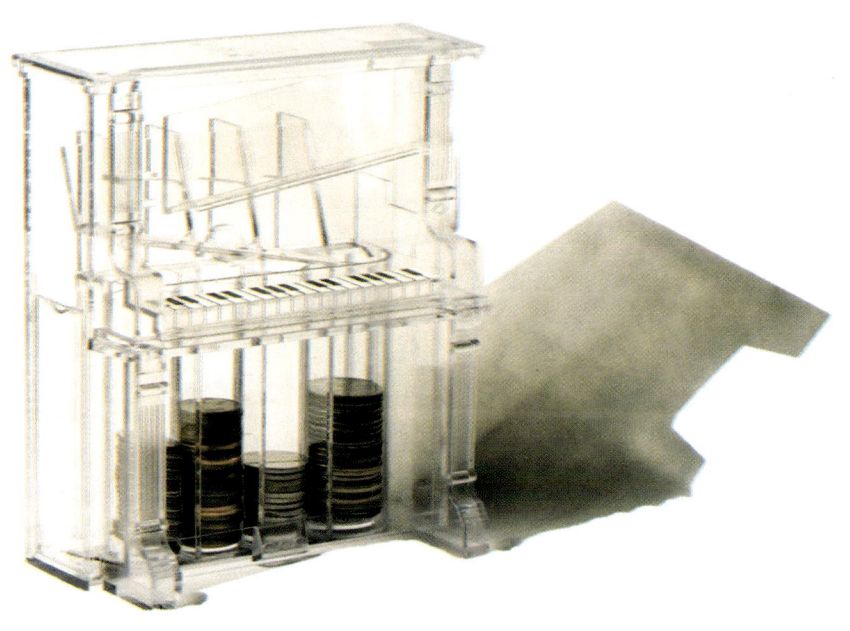

Our piano wasn't just a piano. It was a Gulbransen player piano. Dark oak. Big and heavy. Terrific sound for an upright.

Under the keyboard was a compartment where two pumps lived. These would fold out so you could pump them with your feet and send air columns through hoses to operate the keys and turn the piano roll.

Above the keyboard was another compartment with sliding doors. When you opened them, there was a place near the top to insert a piano roll. Then you would pull the roll's end down like a window shade and attach it to a roller below. With your feet pumping away, the piano roll would move over a drum and its pattern of holes would open or stop air columns to make certain keys play when they were supposed to. The faster you pumped, the faster it would go. I'm sure we had quite a few piano rolls, but the only three I remember are *When my Baby Smiles at Me*, *Stardust*, and Liszt's *Hungarian Rhapsody #2*. I can still hear *When my Baby Smiles at Me* pumped through at about 5 times the right tempo. It was pretty funny, especially when we sang along and changed the word "smile" to "smell."

Logo from an old magazine ad for Gulbransen pianos.

One of my earliest musical memories involved that piano. I was about 5 years old and too small to sit on the stool and reach the foot pumps. At first, I got on the floor and pumped by hand, but that was too much work. So I managed to

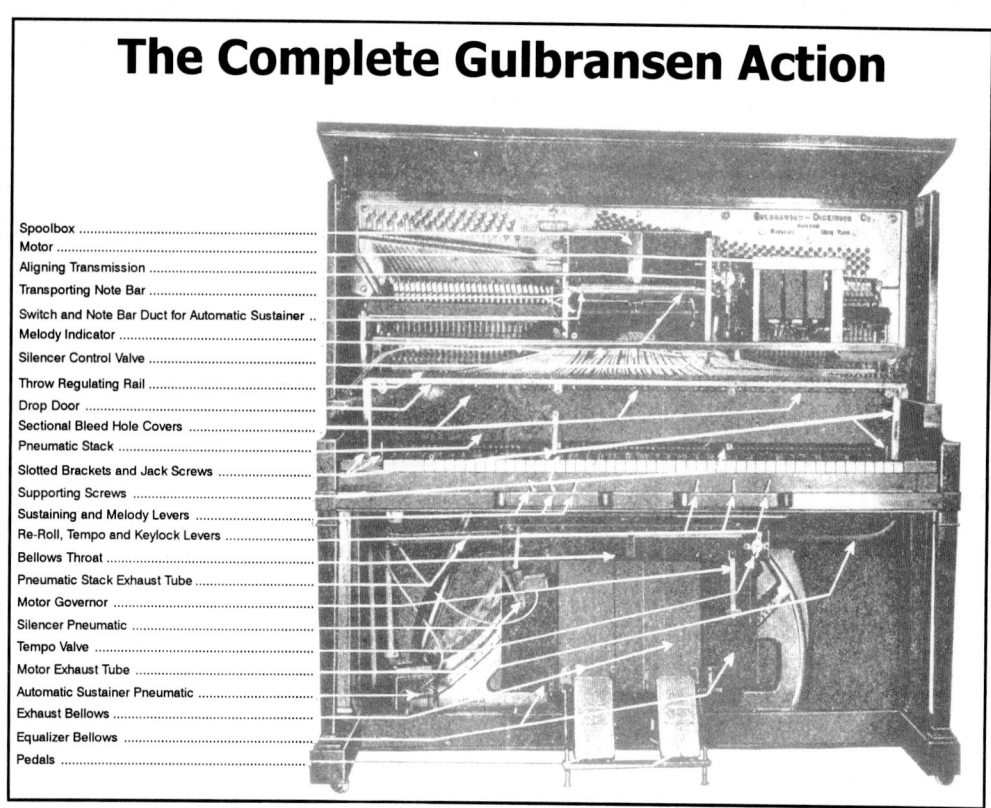

This illustration is from the Gulbransen manual that came with each piano. However, it seems to me that the Silencer Control Valve, the Bleed Hole Covers, and the Jack Screws could also have come from a "Tools for Gangsters" catalogue.

convince my younger sister Janice that pumping those pedals by hand was a lot of fun. (She was so gullible in those days.) She pumped away and loved it. I, meanwhile, sat on the piano stool and pretended I was playing piano.

Years later, when I was in high school and my friend Eddie Dingledy came over to the house to see me one day, he found me "playing" the Liszt. He didn't notice that my fingers didn't hit all the keys that were going up and down. He just assumed that I was really playing it. And he was amazed big time at how well I could play.

The look on his face when I held my hands in the air while the piano kept on playing was the biggest applause for a musical performance that I have ever received.

By the way, that early training I gave Janice on the player piano really paid off for her. It was the very beginning of her successful piano playing career. But has she ever thanked me for starting her on the ground floor and making her work her way up? I don't think so.

The roll-playing part of the piano eventually broke down and we couldn't find anybody to fix it, but the piano itself worked well for years.

Janice practiced on it, hour after hour, year after year.

She accompanied me on it, first for clarinet pieces, then for bassoon, and we mustn't forget all the after-dinner opera singing I did.

The Gulbransen was the center of every family get-together in our house. Not only old Italian songs were sung around it, but also old American songs that you liked to harmonize to—*The Old Mill Stream, Shine on Harvest Moon*—those kinds of songs. Thousands of Christmas carols were sung around that piano. And Latin masses were previewed there so my father would get a feel for them before he introduced them to his choir. Show tunes. Hit tunes. Jazz. Marches. *Slaughter on Tenth Avenue.* Chopin. Verdi. Gershwin. Sinatra. Cole Porter. Stan Kenton. Arias. Silent movie music. Everything. Even "Abbadabadabadaba said the monkey to the chimp...etc."

When Janice married Stu Aubrey and moved to Youngstown, Ohio there were no more pianists left in our house. And since big family meals and celebrations had also moved to Youngstown to be with Janice's new family, or to Evelyn's house to be with hers, there weren't even any visiting piano players.

The big upright took up a lot of space in our small living room and my mother began to see it as a huge dustcatcher. So one day it moved to Evelyn's house on Hazelcroft Avenue.

It wasn't played very much there either. Evelyn had gotten out of the habit and her kids weren't old enough yet.

There came an afternoon when I went to visit Ev and found the piano outside on her porch.

In daylight, you could see all the ring marks from years of wine glasses and pop bottles. And the gouges and scratches and scars caused by various cats, kids and flying toys. The dark oak veneer bubbled here and there, and was chipped here and there. The ivory was very, very yellow.

When I hit a key, the sound was a tiny, tinny whimper.

The piano was old and used up.

It was waiting for the junk man to haul it away.

11
MY LAST CLARINET TEACHER: ALPHONSE DEVIVO

When I was 15 years old, I had gone a whole year without clarinet lessons. Much to my surprise, I began to miss them. I think it had a lot to do with realizing that music-wise, I was becoming the black sheep of my family. Also, most of my friends were still taking lessons and I didn't want to be left behind. But mostly I wanted to get good enough to beat out Johnnie Duff and Bill Brasile for first chair in the high school band.

Somehow I managed to convince my parents that not only was I ready to start lessons again, this time I would practice hours a day, every day including holidays. I would practice so hard that my lips would become strong enough to crack walnuts and my fingers would move so fast that if I wore rings, they'd melt.

Either because my parents didn't want to burden Al Colella with me again or, more likely, Al Colella respectfully refused to be burdened by me again, my new teacher would be Al DeVivo.

I don't want to take anything away from my other cousins, but Alphonse DeVivo was my favorite, the big brother I never had. He was handsome, even-tempered, loved kids and animals, loved jokes and joking around. He was the adult relative I could always talk to as an equal. When I was older and lived in other cities, every time I returned to New Castle for a visit, I'd look to see where Al was playing that weekend and go and catch him. He was always happy to see me.

I used to tell my friends that New Castle was the only city in the world you could go to on any Friday night, and somebody, at some bar, would be playing *Night Train* on a tenor sax. Usually that would have been Al doing the playing. He was wonderful on the tenor sax, made it sound as sweet as an alto when he wanted, or as down and dirty as a baritone.

But he had a way with almost any instrument he played, whatever style he played in.

parents got him ice skates. Not only did he find where they were hidden in the closet a week before Santa would deliver them, but he took them out of the box, went skating, brought them back and returned them to the box without Uncle Tom or Aunt Lizzie ever knowing about it. On Christmas day, he was SO surprised when he opened his present.)

 I loved my lessons with Al DeVivo. They were the first ones I ever had that were fun. The reason they were fun was because Al enjoyed them, too. By the time I started lessons with him, I had already been playing and taking lessons for a number of years so I was no "Twinkle, Twinkle, Little Star" rookie. My fingers knew their way around the keys. This meant that I could get into some fairly sophisticated music and Al managed to find me lots of interesting pieces to study instead of the same old exercises that I had been playing all my life. Much of what he assigned me was the first clarinet parts of clarinet duets. At my lessons, he would accompany me, playing the second clarinet part.

 I don't think he charged my father for my weekly visits. I think the whole reason he gave me lessons was so that he could have somebody to play duets with. Even if it was only me.

12
THE FRIENDLY NATIVES

In case you visit New Castle some day, I don't want you to feel like a stranger. So I've decided to introduce you to a few of its residents. But I want you to know them as we know them, by their nicknames. The following is a list of "Folks You Should Know" compiled for the fun of it a few years ago by my cousins Al DeVivo, Madeline Gurneal, Barbara Zumpella, Vivian Rauso, my Aunt Mary Rauso, and my mother. The nicknames are the ones in bold type.

How were these nicknames arrived at? In many cases, your guess is as good as mine. But sometimes it had to do with physical features, like how big your nose is, or how short, tall, fat, skinny, bald, pimply or cross-eyed you are.

Your profession sometimes named you, for instance there's a whole family of "Shoes" who were shoemakers.

Or perhaps you got your name from an event. This was the case with my cousin Ralphy who was originally nicknamed "Pie" because of his round face. But then one day, while swimming in the quarry he almost drowned. So his pals re-nicknamed him "Glub-Glub" for obvious reasons.

Some of the Italian nicknames can get pretty interesting if you decipher them. For example, "Cagaoglio." We all know what "caga," or "caca" is, don't we? And "oglio" is Italian for "oil." You figure it out.

The important thing to know about these nicknames is that they're only nicknames for a short time and then all of a sudden they become real names. I never knew that "Butter" Priscaro's real first name was Anthony until I read this list. Or that "Cheapasport" even had another name.

To really get a feel for the rhythm of the names, be sure to use the nicknames with their last names when possible. Then Oochiegoote Rozzi, Pastafazool Palmiero, Philomena Papoch and Pie Lombardo start to sound less like characters in The Sopranos, and more like the menu for an Italian dinner.

You don't really have to read this list now. Just cut it out and put it in your wallet so it will be handy when you pass through town.

Folks You Should Know

Alice the Indian, Alice Conti, her son is Tommy Indian
Bananas, Joe Panella
Benny and Lady Duck, Ben Russo and wife
Big Mouth, Joe Russo
Blau, Tony Russo (worked at Simon Blau store)
Blubber, Frank Castrucci
Bluckaboord (blackbird), Mr. and Mrs. Fusco
Boots, Al Russo (the cop)
Butter, Tony Priscaro the drummer
Cagaoglio (caga-olio), Andy Masters
Cheapasport (Cheapsport), John Ciccone whose wife was Annie Cheapasport
Chisel, Sammy Peak
Coal Dock, Domenick DeMarco
Crow, Sam Rozzi
Crow Bait, John Conti
Darky, Louie Domenick
Fatty, Emil Orlando the trumpet player.
Finn or Fizz, Jim Funera
Fracacicce (pronounced fra-ca-chee-che) see Gumshoes
Fridgie, Tom Litera Jr.
Froggie, Rose Orlando
Giovanni Beano (Bee NO), Giovanni Mairano
Giuseppe Neck-a-tie, Giuseppe Pecoraro
Glub-Glub, Ralph Lombardo (See Pie)
Googy, Andy Gangliero
Grub, Albert Panella
Gumshoes, Salvatore Russo
Hammer, Sam Martello the barber
Harpo, Ralph Tommelleo
Jabby, Albert Conti
Jen-nee, Louie Cangey, Jr.
Jit, Jerry Picarro
Joe Bum, Joe Russo whose wife is Rose Bum of course
Lala, Richard Prescaro
La Nenna, Joe Bum's mother
La Sheeny (She-NEE), Jessie Cox
Lindy, Paul Russo who wanted to fly
Marianna Catena, Fracacicce's wife
Mis-dea, Old man Russo
Mouse, Mickey Rauso
Oochiegoote, Mike Rozzi
Pabby, Carmen Conti
Pah-Pah LaPez, John Frank
Paparagiana, Patsy Deluca, a singer
Pastafazool, Louie Palmiero
Pee-Goke (Pea-GOCK, peacock), Bart Lombardo
Peppone, Dom Perrotta who played piano
Philomena Papoch and Papocill, Mrs. Russo and her brother
Pie, Ralph Lombardo
Punkin, Sammy Russo
Quail, Lou Quahliero
Ringey, Oneal Lombardo who played horseshoes
Rosie the Greek, Rose Themos who's husband was Nick the Greek
Running Jim, Jim Leteira
Rupture or Rupp for short, John Masters
Sammy Goose, Sam Russo
Scaboch (Sca-BOCH), Adamo family members
Shanky, Vassily Mutsatsos
Shills, Johnny Diana
Shkagie (shca-GEE), Old man Frank
Shoes, Carmen Pastore
Short Pants, Mrs. Fazio's brother
Shpillapeep (Spillthepipe), Michele Rivezzi, Pete's father
Snake, Domenick Carbone
Spagie (spa-GEE), Tony DeFelice who played trumpet
Spanky, Irma Dottle's sister
Squarehead, Sam DiPiero
Tap-Toe, Johnny Conti
The King, Philomena Papoch's husband
Tomatoes, Patsy Ianotta
Tony O Zoop, Tony Russo
Turtle, Pete Zarilla
U Chooch, Tony Martino
Whisk, Carmen Cardella
Wimpy, Eddie Ezzo
Wrong Way, Jim Cardella
Yonko, John Quahliero
Yummy, Pat Vitale
Zump's, Zumpella's store

13
WHY I SWITCHED FROM CLARINET TO BASSOON

When I entered high school, I was quite comfortable with my musical career. I don't care what anybody says, by then I was a pretty good clarinet player. In spite of a serious lack of practicing, I did quite well when I went up against other players my age. If I wasn't always first chair, I was pretty close. In a musical town like New Castle, with its great clarinet players and teachers, that's not bad.

So I was surprised when Evelyn and her husband Ken suggested that I switch to bassoon. At first, I thought they were crazy. Bassoon? Nobody plays bassoon. No girl dates a bassoon player. Clarinet was in my genes, for goodness sake. And I had just recently graduated from a number 1½ reed to a harder, more professional number 2 reed, a big step in anybody's book. Clearly I was on my way.

On the other hand, except for a couple of days in junior high when Johnny Duff was sick and couldn't play beans, I was never the very best in my age group.

And there were a few guys a bit older than me who were really good, like Tommy Naples (who I was forced to listen to while waiting for my turn to take a lesson from Al Colella. He obviously practiced a whole lot more than me. I hated Tommy Naples.)

And there was this little habit I had of squeaking at every concert I played in.

And there was the way Alphonse would imitate my unique (i.e., bad) sound quality on the clarinet at family gatherings, and everybody would laugh. Even me.

And I was running out of cousin clarinet teachers.

And bassoons don't squeak.

And since there was no other bassoonist in New Castle, I would be the best bassoonist in town!

A no-brainer.

14
MY BUDDY JIM

I officially took up the bassoon the summer before my junior year in high school and immediately became the best bassoonist in New Castle. It felt good while it lasted.

Unfortunately, it lasted only a few weeks. That summer, soon after I made the move from a single to a double reed, the Haven family moved to town from Grand Rapids, Michigan.

Their son, Jim, was my age and had studied the bassoon ever since he was a baby. He was quite accomplished—he had a vibrato and everything.

My options were clear. I could become friends with him. Or I could kill him.

The folks in Yakima, Washington, should thank me on bended knee for choosing the former since Jim eventually became a very good orthopedic surgeon there, specializing in knees. He also served many years on the board of their Yakima Symphony Orchestra.

And I learned to live with being the second best bassoonist in town.

15
THE BASSOON

Very few people have met a real live bassoon. So here's a little help.

Think of the bassoon as the sub-woofer of an orchestra with a tone that's more often felt than heard. You hardly ever hear anybody say, "Hey, did you hear that neat bassoon note?"

The bassoon looks weird because it's really an 8-foot long tube that's doubled into a "U" so it can be played without having other orchestra members tripping over it. Individual notes are achieved through the use of an amazing system of levers and rods. Some of the rods actually travel through the tube so a finger on one side of the bassoon can move keys on the other side. Very often it's the thumb and not a finger that plays the note. In no other wind instrument is the thumb so important.

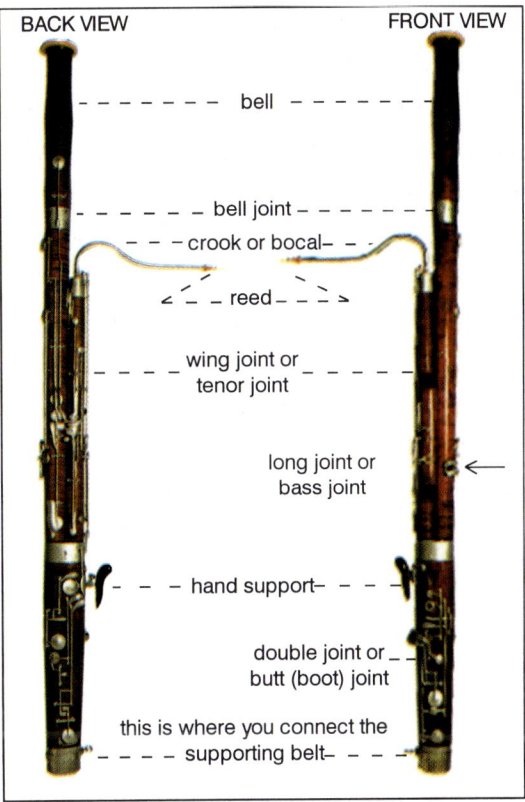

My first bassoon, provided by my school, had somebody's initials carved in its bell. The bassoon in this picture is in good shape.

When you blow into the double reed, the wind column moves through the bocal, then down the tenor joint and one side of the butt joint to the bottom. There, it makes a U-turn and travels up the other side of the butt joint, through the long joint, into the bell joint and out the bell as a note.

The bassoon has a remarkable range—from the B-flat below the staff to a few tones higher than C above middle C. This great range allows the bassoonist to play bass parts and tenor parts, for which he needs to jump between the bass clef and the tenor.

And, as if being saddled with an 8-foot tube, using your thumbs to play so many notes, and jumping between one clef and another isn't enough of a problem, the bassoonist has to contend with yet another hassle—all the notes of every bassoon are out of tune! So, to play in tune, the bassoonist has to adjust the shape and pressure of the mouth on the double-reed differently for each note as it is played. Watch a bassoonist's mouth sometimes as he or she plays a scale. It's an ugly sight. And to think, the bassoonist does this for notes that most people don't even know they're hearing. As far as I'm concerned, all bassoonists are saints.

16
THE *INCOMPLETE METHOD FÜR DIE* HOLZBLASINSTRUMENTE

Around the time I switched to bassoon, I discovered a series of music method books written by a certain Professor Willem Von Schmutzig* who might have been a classmate of P.D.Q. Bach.** The following, from his *Incomplete Method für die Holzbasinstrumente* book, cleared up a lot of confusion in my mind:

Der Woodwind group is divided into three major classifications:
    1. Der Single Reeds,
    2. Der Double Reeds,
    3. Der No Reeds.

---

* "Schmutzig" means "dirty" in German.
** P.D.Q. Bach, the recently discovered black sheep of the Bach family, was a master composer of magnificently mediocre music. His "discoverer" is Professor Peter Schickele who is, among other things, a bassoonist. (That makes four bassoonists you'll meet in this book, five if you count Vic Huff. Some people go their whole lives without meeting one!) Professor Schickele is also a composer who scored one of my favorite science fiction movies, *Silent Running* (starring Bruce Dern and those cute little robots, Huey, Dewey and Louie). He also has a syndicated radio show, The Schickele Mix. And he is the author of arguably the funniest musical bit ever recorded, a performance of Beethoven's Fifth Symphony as if it were a football game with two sports announcers giving us the play-by-play.

    I've never met Professor Schickele so he hasn't paid me for saying these nice things about him. But if he wants to, it's okay with me.

17
VIC HUFF

My first bassoon teacher was Vic Huff, one of those old-time music teachers who, like Alphonse, would work at one of the town's music stores and teach any instrument a parent would pay to have their kids learn. Actually, I think at one time Vic did play bassoon, but I never heard him. His main instrument was clarinet and I guess he was pretty good on it.

My lessons were very strange and filled with a lot of tension that had nothing to do with how little I had practiced or how badly I played. You see, Vic was a huge man. In a town of some extraordinarily large people, which New Castle was, Vic blended in quite nicely. A B-flat clarinet in his hands looked like an E-flat. And in the basement of the music store where I took my $5 lesson in a small windowless room, they had these old rickety chairs with wobbly legs. I was sure that Vic was going to demolish his. I always played with one eye on the music and the other on Vic. If the chair gave way, I sure didn't want to get caught in the avalanche.

But that's not all. Vic always fell asleep during my lessons. He'd point to where he wanted me to start playing and I'd get a couple of measures into the exercise and pretty soon I'd hear this snoring. He'd usually wake up when I stopped playing. But not always. And there I was, stuck, not knowing what to do. Do I wake him up, therefore calling attention to the ludicrousness of these lessons and admitting my own stupidity for paying him the five bucks? Or do I sit there quietly waiting for him to wake up, which is even more stupid? I usually took the middle ground, playing the piece over again as loudly as I could with a big finish. And sometimes I'd keep time with my foot as hard as I could.

Why did I keep taking lessons from Vic? Because he was the only bassoon teacher in town.

18
MY BASSOON CAREER TAKES OFF

There came a time when, to amuse my family, I told them how my bassoon teacher would fall asleep during my lessons.

They were not amused.

Arrangements were soon made for me to take lessons from Ben Spiegel who was a bassoonist with the Pittsburgh Symphony. Wow! This was pretty impressive. Not only because he was with the symphony, but more important, the lessons were $20 an hour. That's in 1950's dollars! Nobody in my family had ever paid that much for a lesson. I don't think anybody in New Castle paid that much for a lesson. This was the big time.

19
MY PITTSBURGH BASSOON LESSONS

Here's how we set it up. My lessons were every other Sunday. I would take an hour train ride to Pittsburgh, catch a bus to Ben Spiegel's apartment for an 11 a.m. lesson, take a bus back and catch the 3 p.m. train home. Sounds easy, right?

Here's how it really went:

Every other Sunday, I would wake up at about 4:50 a.m, which gave me just enough time to scrape the ice off the windshield of my father's Studebaker and drive it to the 5 a.m. mass at Saint Mary's. Since nobody really wanted to be there that early, including the priest, mass usually didn't last more than 20 minutes, only 10 if you left right after communion like me. Then I would drive back home to pick up my father.

My father would then drive me and my bassoon to the train station in Mahoningtown in time to catch the 5:40 train to Pittsburgh, the only choice for Sundays*. It was still dark and there wasn't a lot of traffic in New Castle that early on Sunday, so we never had any trouble making the train. (Come to think of it, there wasn't a lot of traffic in New Castle on any day, at any time.)

Upon arriving in the P&LE train station in Pittsburgh, I would lug my bassoon across the Smithfield Street Bridge which, in winter, was a very cold trip. Can't you just see me, a little guy, all alone, bundled up in his rumpled khaki raincoat with its zipped-in lining, hauling a big bassoon across a wintry wind-swept bridge in early morning half-light in Pittsburgh, Pennsylvania? Sort of tugs the heart, doesn't it?

Once across the bridge, I would head for the only place that was warm and open on Sunday morning, the People's Drug store on Liberty Avenue. There I would peruse all the magazines and books in the periodical section, then sit at

---

*The train ride was a freebie, thanks to a pass my father got for working on the B&O.

the counter and drink coffee until it was time to catch my bus. I still remember those coffee mugs, they were the thick ones that weighed a ton, and you lifted them to drink with both hands for the extra warmth.

After my lessons I would take the bus back downtown and spend a couple of hours walking around waiting for my train. At least, that's what I told my folks. But the truth is that I had discovered the Art Cinema.

The Art Cinema was a movie theater that opened at 1 p.m. on Sundays and showed skin flicks. It was amazing to me how many men wanted to watch porn on a Sunday afternoon, and they all had these long khaki raincoats just like mine. (Maybe they were waiting for trains, too.) Years later, when I was working at an ad agency in Pittsburgh, many of the stores I had come to know during those bassoon lesson days were gone from downtown Pittsburgh. But the Art Cinema was still there.

So, to sum up, those Sundays really went like this: 4:50 am. Wake up. Still dark. Early mass. Leave after communion. Studebaker to station. Empty train. Cold bridge. Check out *Playboy* and *Mad*. Coffee in big mugs. Bus. Lesson. Bus. Dirty movies. Train home.

20
BEN SPIEGEL

In addition to his symphony job, Ben was also a professional photographer, and he gave me the bassoon lessons in his studio/darkroom. He was the first grown man I met who had a work room that wasn't in the basement.

He was a good teacher, and he made me believe that I could be a good bassoonist. And since something told me that Ben wouldn't waste time teaching someone who didn't practice, I actually practiced long hours during the week, and went to these lessons prepared. So, maybe I really was on the road to bassoon stardom.

For the first time, I got to use real bassoon reeds. Like all professional double reed musicians, Ben made his own reeds. He made them for his students, too. He'd have me play several of them until I found the one or two that were absolutely right for me.

I was so happy that I didn't have to buy one of those plastic noisemakers that music stores were selling for bassoon reeds back then. Going into a music store in New Castle and asking for a bassoon reed was as bad as going into a drug store and asking for a condom. You tried to do it when nobody was around to laugh at you or think you were a pervert.

Ben taught me a lot of bassoon. For the first time I began to appreciate the subtleties of the instrument. I was always fascinated by the intricate web of thin rods running through the inside of the instrument, connecting the keys in ways to give optional fingerings to the player. But I never realized that of all the wind instruments, the bassoon's tuning is the least reliable. As I said earlier, every bassoonist has to tune each note individually by making tiny changes to the shape of his embouchure and strength of his wind column. And to make matters worse, every bassoon is different. The next time you hear a bassoonist play an arpeggio, know that he is performing a delicate adjustment on each note that he plays, no matter how fast he plays them. Sure, every great brass or woodwind player does this too, but with a bassoon, you have to do it even if you're not so great. Like me.

He also taught me how to interrupt an interval jump between high and low notes with a quick flick of a thumb or index finger key. If you did it well enough, this would be imperceptible to a listener, and it would break the air column just enough to let you complete the leap of notes without scratching the sound.

One of the most important things he taught me was that you don't have to waste energy looking good in order to actually be good. This happened at one lesson while I was playing a piece I really liked. I had practiced hard on it and knew it well. So, during my lesson, to show Ben that I knew it well, I let myself be swept up in the beauty of my own sound and euphorically waved my elbows up and down in time with the music, dramatizing, emphasizing, and otherwise underlining the glory of it all. Ben's comment was something to the effect of "What the hell are you doing? Are you trying to fly?" When I explained to him that I was "feeling" the music, he told me that elbows don't feel, and never do that again.

One of the best days of my young life was the day Ben and his wife asked me to stay for lunch after my lesson. I remember his wife as being thin, pretty and cheerful and she was also an artist. Can you imagine how awesome it was for a high school kid from New Castle to have a Sunday lunch with his teacher who was a symphony musician, and his wife who was an artist, in a big city apartment where all the rooms were on the same floor? Can you imagine how grown up and sophisticated I felt?

Okay, the lunch was some strange salad thing with mayonnaise and nuts in it, and there was something fishy, maybe salmon, that wasn't cooked very well, but so what? Except for the lack of pasta, this was the way life should always be!

21
LAST LESSON IN PITTSBURGH

I only took lessons from Ben during my junior year in high school. The lessons stopped when summer started.

That was when the Pittsburgh Symphony's season was over, and when Ben and his wife made their annual trek to Lake Chautauqua, in western New York State. The Chautauqua Institution had a special summer music program. Many students and teachers spent pleasant cultural summers there, learning, teaching and performing. Ben played in the Chautauqua Symphony and taught.

Before he left, Ben told me all the great plans he had for me. He said that I had talent enough, that he would teach me enough, and that he had friends enough to get me an audition at the Curtis Institute. He was sure I could get a full scholarship there, no sweat. And further, he was sure that I would be able to get into the Pittsburgh Junior Symphony for the coming year. He gave me books of music to work on all summer while he was gone, so we could get a running start when he got back. Oh my God, could all this happen to me? Was I really going to grow up to be a musician?

But then, this was summer.

Ah, summers when you're a teenager. Do you remember them?

This was the summer of 1955, my last high school summer. I was 17. My pimples were fading. My testosterone was flowing. I was licensed to drive the Studebaker. And heck, my lessons didn't start until September. I'd start practicing next week. I really would.

But I didn't. I never cracked one of those books all summer long. And after goofing off all summer, how could I go back to this guy who had made all these great plans for me? How could I tell him that I didn't practice, never, not once, all summer long?

I was truly ashamed of myself and I never went back. I never even called him.

But I did see Ben again.

Somewhere along the line, Ben had decided to leave the Symphony and become a full-time professional photographer. Years later, when I worked for an advertising agency in Pittsburgh, I saw him at an advertising show and got up the courage to go and talk to him. It was going to be one of the most difficult things I ever had to do, but I really wanted to apologize and ask his forgiveness.

He didn't remember me.

22
A POEM FROM THE 60'S BY ME

The Bassoonist

The thing a bassoonist does

is sit there in his section,

with his cumbersome, ugly,

joke of a musical instrument.

And softly he billows his pillows of sound.

More often than not,

he's overshadowed by gangs of strings.

Or buried beneath a bravado of brass.

But he has his moments.

Moments of laughter.

Moments of intrigue

And, oh those long, painful moments accompanying

Strauss and Berlioz heroes

to their deaths.

continued

But usually

his soft voice blends into the world,

indistinguishable, yet there,

needed for his character,

for his particular brand of beauty.

What this world needs are more bassoonists.

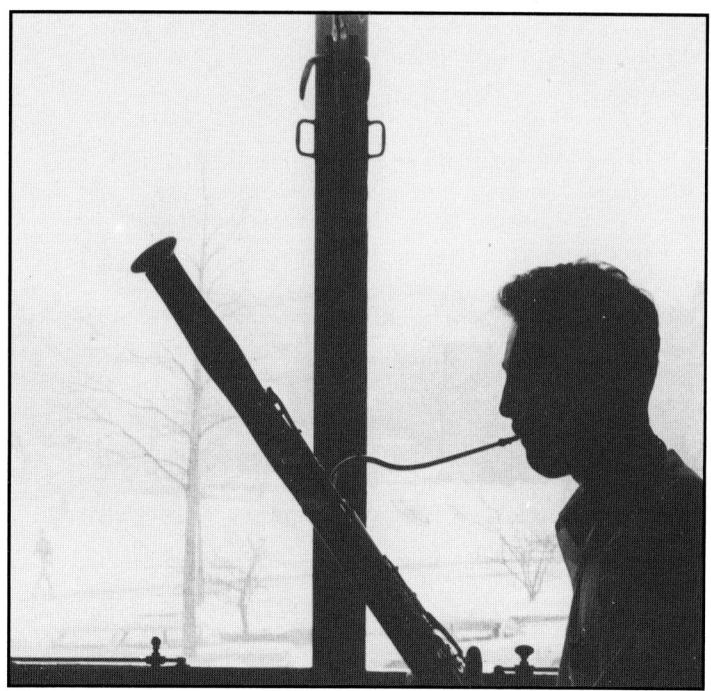

A picture I took of my friend, Mark Wilde, at Penn State.

23
BAND IS KING

There was one oddity in this musical environment that I grew up in. For a town that was as musical and as Italian as ours, I now find it quite amazing that we grew up knowing so little about opera.

Oh, opera music was all around us. New Castle loved Mario Lanza and worshiped Saint Enrico. And yes, we knew arias and overtures. But to most of us (except for my bathroom-cleaning sister and Aunt Jenny who for some reason had memorized every single story of every opera ever written), those arias were just Italian songs. And the overtures were what you heard between the marches at a band concert. They had no other context! The *Poet and Peasant* was not an opera, it was a band number. The *William Tell Overture* was not only the beginning, but also the end of it. There was no more. Verdi was wonderful, of course, but we knew him only by the bits and pieces of his work.

It never occurred to me, until Aunt Jenny set me straight, that this was actually how most of Italy got to know Verdi and other composers. She reminded me that when those guys were writing their operas, there was no radio, no TV, no records, no CDs or tapes or film. And since only the very big cities had the theaters and the wherewithal to stage a big production, the rest of Italy never got to see an opera. Not ever. But they did get to know the stories and music through the grapevine. Aunt Jenny said that actors and singers, either alone or in small troupes, would travel the countryside, stop in the small villages and put on a show for the entertainment-starved citizens. They'd tell the plots of the latest operas, I suspect with great Italian flair, and sing a few arias. And that's how 99% of the Italians learned to love opera. In bits and pieces. Who knew?

The only opera I know that ever came to New Castle was a black and white film version of *I Pagliacci*. Even that didn't come all the way into town. It played at the local drive-in on Route 224. My father loaded the family in the Studebaker, and took us to see it. Boy, was that clown depressing.

Here and there, kids took violin lessons but they usually ended up as drummers, cymbalists and glockenspielists in the bands. My cousin Vito was a violinist, but played drums in the Blue Coat Band and string bass for dance bands. At one time there was a New Castle Symphony Orchestra, but it didn't last as long as Wagner's Ring Cycle.

In New Castle, band was king. For most of us, if it didn't have a spit valve or a reed, it didn't count. We loved band music. We loved uniforms. We loved a parade.

24
A DIGRESSION

Jump ahead a few years.

In the late '90s, my wife Judy and I found out what all the shouting was about and discovered the joy of opera. With our friends Dan and Sherry Heagy, we saw *Turandot* (the one with the sets designed by David Hockney) at Chicago's Lyric Opera and fell in love with it. The four of us immediately signed up for season tickets.

During our first year of opera going, we found out about opera seating. Up until then, we were such innocents. We knew nothing about "seat envy." Nobody told us the basic "Rule of the Rows" that no matter which row your seat is in, you will pity all those who sit behind you and hate everybody who sits in front of you. But we're quick learners. During the intermission of the second opera of our season, we saw an art director we knew, but didn't like much, strut oh so smugly down to a seat ten rows ahead of us. That's when we began to hate our seats.

Thus we joined in the fierce competition that goes on each year when opera goers sign up for the following year's opera series. Each year we checked the box that asked us if we wanted to change our seats. Yes. And we checked the box that asked us if we wanted to make a bribe...er..I mean donation to the Lyric. You bet.

We actually did pretty well for beginners. We made slow but steady progress toward the stage, each year gaining more people to be pitied, each year diminishing our supply of people to hate. But last year, we hit the wall. We didn't move at all! We were so depressed.

Obviously, merely checking boxes wasn't going to do the trick. Extraordinary measures were called for. So I wrote a letter to Susan Mathieson, Director of Marketing & Communications at the Lyric. It's my understanding that she also has a lot to do with the seating. The letter's on the next page. Do you think it'll work?

Dear Susan:

I know (because you told me in our recent telephone conversation) that the audience for our Lyric Opera series, F, is a very stable one. And the chances of the four people in our group moving to seats closer to the stage are not very great, even with our usual annual donations.

However, in a blatant attempt to influence what I'm sure is a fair and impartial system of seat assigning, I'd like to tell you about a special problem we've run into in our present seats.

It's "Big Head."

Well, that's what we call him. If you can, imagine Charlie Brown all grown up and sitting very erect in front of you... Wait, better yet, think about those big balloons in the Macy Thanksgiving Day parade. Now you begin to get the picture.

The strange thing is that when you see him at intermission, and you're not directly behind him, he looks normal. But once he gets in that seat, it's like those car seats that adjust as soon as you sit in them. Sproing! Up he pops like the Pillsbury Doughboy. It was my turn to sit behind him for *The Magic Flute*. You know that orange ball thing on top of the pyramid in the background? That's about all that I saw of the opera, the orange ball above the back of his head.

And there's another thing. He has perfect timing. When he leans to the left, deftly encouraging you to lean to the right so you have a small hope of seeing around him, *he somehow knows exactly when you finally get a peek at the stage*! That's when he leans back the other way! So you have swing to the left! Of course, every time you move your head, the people on either side of you also have to adjust! Which means the people in the row behind you have to adjust also! And the people in the row behind them! And so on, all the way back! Until the whole audience behind Big Head's row is adjusting! The effect is not unlike The Wave we see at football games.

Perhaps I exaggerate.

I'm sure he's a very nice man, and he has every right to his own seat at the opera. He can't help the size of his head. I certainly feel sorry for his mother when he was born, I bet she was very, very sore for a long, long time. And he probably has his own problems, like needing a team of barbers for his hair cuts, and having to pay for custom-made 20-gallon Stetsons when he goes to a dude ranch.

But what's fair is fair. We think this is an excellent time for us to push on (and for someone else to get the Big Head seat). Any help you can give us will be greatly appreciated.

Sincerely,

Joe

Joe DeVivo

P.S. If you check out our present seat assignments and figure out who the gentleman is and if he turns out to be a good, personal friend of yours or, God forbid, a relative, *please disregard this letter.*

P.P.S. I realize that the problem can be solved by moving our seats backwards. Forget it!

25
THE NEW CASTLE SYMPHONY

Okay. There was a symphony orchestra in town, but....

In its review of the debut of the New Castle Symphony Orchestra in 1949, our local newspaper, the *New Castle News* proclaimed it "...a much needed vitamin in our cultural diet."

Like many diets, this one didn't last long. Only two years. But that was long enough for my sister Evelyn to meet the French horn player she later married. Vito finally got a chance to play his violin in public. And some pictures were taken that show some of the people I talk about in this book (see next page).

Anthony Casbero conducts the New Castle Symphony Orchestra, about 1950. Photo courtesy of Mrs. Genevieve Casbero.

The New Castle Symphony woodwind section. From left, Mike Prescaro, Al Colella, John Buonpane, Anita DeVivo, Joan Elder, and Roger Pecano. Pianist Edwin Lewis is in the background. Photo from the DeVivo Archives.

26
THE MARCH BEGINS

The first band I joined was at the Mahoningtown school when I was in third grade. I was only in it one year, so all I remember is our uniform was a black cape and my band teacher's name was Miss Thomas who became Mrs. Polland when she got married (teachers didn't have first names in those days).

The next year, after my family moved to New Castle's North Hill, I went to Highland Avenue grammar school. Highland didn't have a band, it only had a "get-together" with a visiting teacher once a week. She got together all the kids who were taking lessons and had us play stuff that even the worst students could play. Since I had been taking lessons for a couple years by now, and most of the others were raw beginners, this was the one time in my life when I was far ahead of my peers. I was clearly the best they had. Even so, I hated it. The music we played was boring. And, oh my God, we sounded awful.

In seventh grade I graduated to George Washington Junior High School which had a real band with real uniforms and everything. Mr. Paton was the conductor and I immediately established myself as one of the better clarinet players there. Okay, a 9th grader held first chair, but I knew that was just a fluke because she was a girl and girls don't play clarinet, they play piano. And besides, she was graduating at the end of the year.

The main thing I learned in the Washington Junior High band was how hard it is to play a clarinet while marching outside in sub-zero weather. Your hands get so cold it's hard to move your fingers as fast as you want. And you lose feeling in your fingertips so you don't really know if you're covering all the holes. And the metal keys freeze up and don't bounce back like they should. And sometimes, your mouth wants to stick to the mouthpiece. Sure, it would be nice to wear thick furry gloves to keep your hands warm, but of course thick gloves won't let you cover the holes so you'll just squeak as you march. The best you can do is wear thin cotton gloves with the fingertips cut out. But they don't help much.

All in all, for cold weather parading, I recommend playing a brass instrument (just three keys, no holes to cover), especially a trombone (no keys, no holes). Or, better yet, drums (no keys, no holes, no metal parts, no staying in tune problems, and the sticks can be used for kindling).*

---

*Yes, it's true that when it rains, a drum's skin will sag and you get a thud when it's played. So what? That's why rim shots were invented.

27
NE-CA-HI

After ninth grade, I graduated to New Castle High School, or Ne-Ca-Hi as it was known by the natives. Our music teacher was Mr. Keene. We used to call him "Stumpy" Keene for some forgotten reason.

Mr. Keene was not well liked. I'm not proud of all the scorn and hate we heaped upon him, but we did have our reasons. First of all, in a town filled with music of all kinds, he remained remarkably aloof for the head of the instrumental music department of the town's only high school. He had nothing to do with the New Castle musical scene. He didn't belong to any band, orchestra or choir in town, not even one of the non-Italian ones. He never shared any of our musical experiences outside of school.

Also, with so many relatives and neighbors being such good musicians, we had enough musical heroes. Since he was so different from them—I don't think *La Forza del Destino* was part of his vocabulary—he became the anti-hero, the enemy.

And finally, and worst of all, he took the fun out of music for us. As every music teacher knows, young kids in a band want to blast out and blow their audiences away. But a good music teacher helps them discover there's more to life than *fortissimo* without smothering that passion.

Mr. Keene smothered it. He was so insistent on his *pianissimos* that they became the focus of every rehearsal, every concert. Somehow, the music got lost in the struggle to tame his wild horses. There was no life left, no joyful sound in what we played.

But let's be fair. It's quite possible that Mr. Keene had some personal problems at home that took up so much time he couldn't get involved with the community, even if he wanted to. And maybe no outsider, no matter how smart and talented, would have stood a chance of winning a share of our adulation away from the homegrown superstars. And maybe he actually was very nice and helpful to some of the other kids, just not to me and my friends. And, okay, maybe it is a real possibility that we just played too goddam loudly all the time and not only did it drive Mr. Keene nuts, he knew it would be better for us to learn to control ourselves and that we would be better musicians for it.

But it would take so much fun out of my memories to be that compassionate, that understanding.

28
FRIDAY NIGHT FOOTBALL

The most important performances the Ne-Ca-Hi band gave were during the Friday night football games.

In New Castle, as in many smaller towns across the county, the high school football game was the biggest athletic event a sports enthusiast could attend. You didn't even have to have a kid enrolled there. If you graduated from New Castle High School, and everybody in New Castle either graduated from there, or was going to, you cared about the football team. The whole town was focused on those games. People planned their lives around them. They met old friends and classmates there. Old men rehashed the games at the plant and in the barber shop. New Castle vs. Sharon was as big as Green Bay vs. Chicago. The local high school coach was as big as Mike Ditka.* And if the team lost, the whole town felt bad for a week.

So, to say that the football games were our most important band gigs is not an overstatement.

The roar of the crowd as we marched onto the field just before the game started was deafening. We would march onto the field playing the New Castle High Fight Song. We'd play a few bars of melody and then everybody in the stands shouted "Fight! Fight! Fight!" hysterically. And then we played a few more bars of melody and everybody screamed "Ella-ka-nee-kanack-kanack!" even more

---

* Former Chicago Bears coach Mike Ditka came from Aliquippa, Pennsylvania, a steel town just a few miles south of New Castle. Since he's about my age and New Castle High often played Aliquippa High in football, chances are pretty good that he played in New Castle's stadium at the very same time I was playing in the band there. Speaking of Aliquippa, a friend of mine, Ted Naron, reminded me that another famous person grew up there. Henry Mancini. His father was a flautist, but Henry, disobeying the natural sex discrimination laws of Italian music, took up the piano. My friend Ted, who is a great music reviewer and critic, said, "...there's no question that even though piano was his instrument, the band culture of Western Pennsylvania was what inspired him to arrange for band as a teen, then later for orchestra. If it weren't for Aliquippa, the world may never have heard *Moon River, Days of Wine and Roses*, the theme to the *Pink Panther* and a whole lot more."

hysterically. (Why Ella-ka-nee-kanack-kanack? I have no idea. Unless it has to do with all the N's and C's in it.) Then we'd do the "Fight! Fight! Fight" thing again. And then, at the end of the song everybody yelled, "A boomerang, a boomerang, a sis boom bah! New Castle High School. Rah! Rah! Rah!" I don't know why. They just did. Then we repeated the whole thing over and over again ad infinitum, or until we got to our formation in front of the flag pole.

Then the flag was raised and we played the *The Star-Spangled Banner*. Then everybody cheered again, hysterically, and we marched off playing the Fight Song again.

At half time we came out and did some formations and fancy marching. For our finale, we formed a big N and C and played the *Alma Mater*. Everybody stood and sang.

During the game we also played marches and other numbers, but we were seated in the end zone and playing so *pianissimo*, I'm sure nobody heard them.

With some minor variations—different music, different letters, different formations—this routine was pretty much the same one followed by every high school and college marching band in the country.

It was almost a religious ritual. Just like a Catholic Mass. People knew when to stand up and sit down. People sang the same songs every week. And lots of it was in a language that nobody understood.

I asked Tommy Zumpella, the cousin who's now head of the band department at New Castle High, to send me the first clarinet part of the Ne-Ca-Hi Fight Song. I never knew that it was the trio of the *Our Director* march!

29
THE STAR-SPANGLED BANNER

I was very fortunate with all the bands I played in. Every one of my band leaders, even Stumpy Keene, felt that *The Star-Spangled Banner* should be played in an efficient manner at a brisk march tempo. None of them believed that it should be over-dramatized, drawn-out, that it should take forever to finish like some bands like to play it. Let me tell you, when you're out there on a football field in sub-zero weather freezing your cotton-covered fingers off, not to mention some other body parts, you really appreciate an efficient, brisk national anthem.

On the next page is a special version of the national anthem. I don't know the author, or who sent it to me, but thanks to both.

The Star-Spangled Banner—a Drummer's Perspective

Oh, say can you Boom, Crash
By the dawn's early Boom, Crash
What so proudly we Boom, Crash
At the twilight's last gleaming
Whose broad stripes and bright Boom, Crash
Through the perilous Boom, Crash
O'er the ramparts we Boom, Crash
Were so gallantly streaming 3 &
1…2…3…
2…2…3…
3…2…3…
4…2…3…
5…2…3…
6…2…3…
7…2…3…
8…2…oh,
Boom Boom Boom
Boom Boom Boom
Boom Boom Boom
Boom Booooommmm; Boom
Boom Boom Boom
Boom Booooommmm; Boom
Boom Boom Boom
Booooooooooooom!

30
OF RED COATS AND BLUE COATS

New Castle is blessed with two Italian bands, the Red Coat Band and the Blue Coat Band. And like Chicago with the Cubs and White Sox, it is a cross-town rivalry. You can't be loyal to both.

The Red Coat Band, or *La Banda Rossa*, is a descendant of the Duke of Abruzzi Band which was started just around the time my father was born, near the beginning of the 20th century. The St. Margaret's Blue Coat Band, or *La Banda Vestita D'Azzurro di Santa Margherita*, is not a descendant of any band. The St. Margaret's Club in Mahoningtown just wanted a band of their own. Or so they said. I bet there was some clashing of egos among the town's musicians that had something to do with it, too.

If you're at all interested in Italian-American bands, get a terrific little book, *Italian Wind Bands, A Surviving Tradition in the Milltowns of Pennsylvania*, by Emma Scogna Rocco. It tells you everything there is to know about them. And it has some awesome pictures, many of them like the one shown here. There's a

La Banda Vestita d'Azzuro in front of St. Margaret's Club about 1919. Photo from the DeVivo Archives.

[handwritten annotations on photo: Pop / Mike Prescaro / Director Louis Gaspare / Uncle Tom]

really good one of my cousin Louie on page 128. (As mentioned before, Louie, or "Junior" as we called him, is Al Colella's kid brother and probably the greatest of all the great clarinet players in New Castle. I'd put him up against any clarinetist, anywhere.) Also, check out page 166. It's a hilarious picture of what looks like everybody who couldn't get a date for the prom that year.

In my memory, the Red Coats and Blue Coats were big rivals, competing for the same saints' day gigs among the area's churches and religious clubs. And of course, each thought it was better than the other. If you were Italian, you didn't play in both. On the other hand, there were a few non-Italian musicians who could merrily flit from one band to the other at will. Nobody cared about them.

Ken, my brother-in-law, took me to the Red Coat Band and I spent the summer of '55 playing bassoon with them under the direction of Bebe (pronounced "B.B.") Biondi who had been its director for 41 years. Bebe was well known in New Castle politics, a Republican big shot who could dispense favors, so he was a popular guy. As smart as he was, he never learned to drive. His son was his chauffeur.

Rehearsals were on the second floor of the Sons of Italy Club. On the first day I rehearsed with them, I got a lot of stares when I began to put my bassoon together. I think it was the first time many of them had seen one up close and personal. That's when I first heard the "farting bedpost" line.

I don't think the band ever expected to have a bassoonist, because there were very few bassoon parts to the music they played. Most of the time, I played the baritone horn part which ironically was often a transcription from the bassoon part in the original symphonic arrangement. It didn't matter that much since I don't think anybody ever heard me. There's a lot more passion than *pianissimo* in an Italian band, and the mellow sounds of a bassoon didn't stand a chance.

The Red Coat Band in the 50s. Photo from the DeVivo Archives.

    I also rehearsed with the Blue Coat Band a couple of times that year, but even though I had more cousins in the Blue Coat Band than in the Red Coats, I felt a little dirty. After all, the Red Coat Band was my first.

    The last I heard, my cousin Tommy Zumpella is now directing the Red Coats. And my cousin Vito's son, David Colella, is directing the Blue Coats.

31
FEASTING

Summer was the time of celebrations. We're not talking here of generic celebrations like wedding anniversaries or graduations. In New Castle, the word "celebration" meant one thing only, a street fair sponsored by a church or club, usually in honor of a Catholic saint, around the time of that saint's "feast day." It took place outdoors on closed-off streets or on an empty lot and it featured food, bingo, a few rides for the kids, pitch-a-penny and spinning wheel gambling games, parades, band concerts and fireworks. Oh yes, on a saint day there would be a mass, and a procession of the band with a statue of the saint.

The St. Margaret's Club and the St. Vitus Church threw the big celebrations in New Castle, but there were also saint's day celebrations all over western Pennsylvania, eastern Ohio and West Virginia.

The Italian bands were a major part of the celebrations.

For instance, the St. Margaret's celebration was kicked off early on a day around the 20th of July with the Blue Coat band marching through the neighborhood. Well, calling it "marching" is really a stretch. There were a lot of overweight, old guys in that band. The uniforms were wool, it was summer and marching was for soldiers and school kids anyway. What this band did was sort of stroll, sometimes even in time to the music.

At least, that's how they started out. You see, it was traditional for them to make frequent stops along the way, usually at the front yards of friends and relatives, and play special requests. As their reward, or enticement, they were usually offered a glass of homemade wine or a shot of whiskey with an Iron City* chaser. Which they accepted, just to be sociable. At every stop.

Since there were lots of friends and relatives along the way, their stops were many. So, by the time they got to our house, which was near the edge of town,

---

*I'm sure other beers were drunk, but it was usually an Iron City (or an "Arn" in Western-Pennsylvania-speak.) The whiskey was usually Seagram's 7.

uniform jackets were unbuttoned, band hats pushed back, neckties untied, a shirttail or two were hanging out and the musicians were doing more weaving than strolling.

The summer I played for the Red Coat Band, I found that they did things differently for the St. Lucy's celebration in Hillsville, Pennsylvania.* The town is just west of New Castle and, as its name promises, it's filled with many steep hills. Instead of marching up and down those hills, the band rode on a flat-bed truck. Take it from me, that truck was a good idea. With the age, weight and cholesterol intake of the average Italian band member, they would have dropped like flies on those hills. But while it was a lot easier on the band, there was none of the stopping and socializing. So it lacked the personal touch and free booze of the St. Margaret's parade.

In the evening of a celebration, there would always be a band concert. The program would usually feature a lot of Italian overtures— Verdi and Rossini were very big—and Italian marches. (I remember when I was 7 or 8 years old, I'd go behind the bandstand where nobody could see me and conduct the *Poet and Peasant* and *William Tell*. I learned every cue, every grand pause, every change in tempo.) But there would also be a lot of Sousa, Strauss and show tunes. There'd be soloists, often a clarinetist playing Weber's *Concertino* or a trumpeter playing *Carnival of Venice* variations. And there would be traditional digressions like when a group of musicians broke off from the big band and played offstage in a sort of duet with the main band.

---

*Hillsville is such a small town, not even on most maps, that you'd think nothing much ever happened there. You'd be wrong. In the 20's, a school for assassins was established in Hillsville. No kidding.

After the concert, the band had one more job to do. They had to lead everybody down to the place where the fireworks would be set off and then play marches and mazurkas between explosions and during the ground displays. And then march back.

It was a long day.

32
FEAST FOOD

Many times in New Castle it was difficult to separate the food from the music. They were the two things in town, besides God, that were supremely important and were everywhere you went. Especially at celebrations.

When I started wrting this I could remember the meatball sandwiches and sausage sandwiches and pizza by the slice sold at celebrations, but I couldn't remember the name of the beans they sold there. So I e-mailed cousin Ralphy who has eaten more Italian food than anybody I know. His answer was a little more than I asked for:

> The beans were lupini, but we called them "lubeens." As for the other food, some years there was fried or roasted chicken. Sometimes there was *pizza cu'gli veerds* (pizza with greens). Suzy Cangey made them best, but mine are pretty good if and when I have both the time, and inclination (and the proper greens are available). The celebration is the first place I ever ate french fries with vinegar. They were served in a cone-shaped cup. You could get beer and wine in the clubhouse. But if you wanted water, you had to get it at the little fountain on the corner of Liberty Street. There was always homemade style pizza—thick slices and square shape. Cotton candy was the only other "Midigun"[American]* food I remember besides the fries. They had no hot dogs or burgers. If you wanted them, you went across the street to the G&H. There may have been popcorn. In fact, now that I think on it, I'm sure. I remember some guys would take empty popcorn boxes, put bricks in them and leave them on the sidewalk. They knew people

---

* The best way to pronounce "American" the Italian way is to leave off the "A," make the "e" sound like the "i" in "bit," change the the "r" to a soft "d," give the "a" an "uh" sound and accent the last syllable, as in midi-GUN. It's the Italian word for "WASP," macaroni and cheese, or any other non-ethnic person, food or thing. The Neapolitan/Casertan Italians often drop syllables in their words, more often at the end than at the front. Giuseppe becomes Giusepp, DeVivo becomes DeVeeve or DeViv, spaghetti becomes spaghett.

liked to kick empty popcorn boxes. Come to think of it, those guys were you and me!

When Vicki and I lived in St. Louis, we went to an Italian celebration on the Hill, home of Joe Garagiola and other baseball players. They had indoor facilities where you could eat a sit-down spaghetti-and-meatball dinner. Absolutely the worst. In fact, I don't think there is any good Italian food in St. Louis. Vicki and I used to drive to Pittsburgh to buy eighteen half-baked pizzas at Mineo's, then freeze them at her parents' place and take them back to St. Louis. The first decent pizza I ever found in Missouri was in Columbia at the Green Pepper Pizza. There are rumors of good Italian in Kansas City, but to me they are unfounded. If I went to K.C. it would be to eat barbecue at Arthur Bryant's.

33
NUMBER 59

Do you remember that old joke about the joke-tellers' convention? Everybody there was so familiar with jokes, that instead of going through the trouble of telling a whole joke, they'd just yell out a number that represented the joke. People would either laugh or not, depending on whether they heard it before.

That joke always reminded me of the Red Coat and Blue Coat bands. They played many old marches that were written by one of the earliest directors of several New Castle Italian bands, Professor Ralph Gaspare, or marches that were brought over from the old country. Somewhere along the line, these marches lost their titles. Or they never had them to begin with. They just had numbers. But the bands had been playing them for so many years, that the audience came to know the marches by those numbers, and requested them by shouting out a number. Just like the joke.

Number 59 was my favorite.

I always thought it would be interesting to make a record featuring those marches. Can you imagine what the label would look like?

The Red Coat Band Plays the Numbers!

Cuts:

1. *26*   5. *52*

2. *93*   6. *44*

3. *7*   7. *30*

4. *9*   8. *59*

Featuring their hit single "59"

34
FIREWORKS!

Fireworks were taken very seriously in New Castle. Still are. Zambelli's of New Castle had grown to be one of the major fireworks companies in the world, responsible for some of the biggest fireworks shows in the country, including Fourths of July in Washington D.C., New York and Chicago. The Vitale, Rozzi and Fazzoni families have also been big New Castle names among those who supply noise and light to the nation.*

But a significant percentage of all their product is exploded right in their own back yard. If you add up all the area's saints' days and other church-sponsored street fairs, throw in some Sons of Columbus, Sons of Italy and Garibaldi Club feasts plus the Fourth of July, you'll find that a lot of fireworks are shot off in and around Western Pennsylvania each year. I remember counting 30 fireworks displays that I personally went to in a single year.

Naturally, the people from New Castle are fireworks connoisseurs. We tend to critique every exploding flower, sparkly shower, whirling pinwheel and zapping light trail. We are strict judges of the precision and rhythm of a presentation. And if it's not loud, it doesn't count.

The fireworks shows in New Castle are no sissy, pit-pit-pit puff stuff you get in towns too afraid to wake up babies and old people. Instead, you get powerful BadaBadaBadaBOOM! window-rattlers that dare you to watch without putting your hands over your ears. I remember when I was a kid, the macho thing to do

---

*The Pyrotechnic Guild International recently held its 25th annual convention in New Castle. The highlights included (1) the traditional Italian "Baby Doll Dance" in which two 12-foot tall puppets spout fireworks from their hands and heads, and finally their heads explode; (2) the *Stars and Stripes Forever* played by specially tuned pyrotechnic whistles; (3) a barrage of 700 titanium salutes; (4) a salute to deceased members of the Guild featuring the launching of a shell containing the ashes of one former member; (5)A Guinness-Book-record-setting Super String of 5.3 million firecrackers bundled together, hung from a crane and then set off by a member who paid $5200 for the privilege, and (6) for the final pop, a gargantuan 36-inch shell, the largest ever fired in North America.

was get as close as possible to where they were setting off the fireworks, and see how long you could go without covering your ears. If you got close enough, you could feel the sudden, quick rush of air that the big explosions sent out.

At the St. Margaret's celebration, the end of the band concert was the signal that it was time for the fireworks. It was the band's job to lead all the people down Liberty Street to the big field near the Pennsy Railroad yard where the fireworks would be shot off.

This was not a simple little parade. The Blue Coats would divide into two smaller bands and while both little bands marched to the field, they'd play a piece named *La Risponda* (The Response).* Few people knew it by that name. We just called it *The Fireworks March*. This is a catchy march where the band in front would play a verse, and then the band behind would "respond" to it with its own verse. Then the front band would answer, and so on.

Everybody knew that music by heart, even the people who never played a musical instrument, and they'd often sing along with the band. I'm sure if the band had ever tried to play something else, there'd have been a riot. During the fireworks show, the band would get itself back together and play marches during pauses. And they'd also play something appropriate for ground displays, like *Anchors Aweigh* for a destroyer shooting fiery Roman-candle bursts from its cannons. Or *Stars and Stripes* for a sparkling, smoking, red, white and blue American flag.

---

* There's a bit of confusion here. *La Risponda* is the name Ralphy gave me. But Tommy Zumpella sent me a piece of music called *Il Bersagliere (The Sharp Shooters)* by Edoardo Boccalare, written in 1908, which is obviously the same as the *Fireworks March* I grew up with. I intend to get to the bottom of this. In the meantime, I find it ironic that *Il Bersagliere* was the name of a crack Italian strike force who marched at running speed, while the marching style of the bands who played this music in New Castle could best be described as "shuffling along," sort of in time to the music.

Of course everybody said "Oooooh" a lot during the show. And after it was all over they'd all say, "It was louder last year."

And everybody would go home satisfied and tired, especially the band.

35
THE FOLLANSBEE GIG

In Follansbee, West Virginia, on every first Saturday in August, the Garibaldi Club had a celebration in honor of their namesake, Giuseppe Garibaldi, the man responsible for unifying Italy, as much as was possible, in the nineteenth century (at about the same time Americans were fighting the Civil War).

I never went to Follansbee myself, but Ralphy went as a member of the Blue Coats. He told me the story about a command that was given before parades that was a bit unusual. I thought I'd let him tell you about it, just like he told me...

> To get there on time, we'd have to get on the bus in New Castle at 4 a.m., Saturday morning. Mike Zumpella, who was the band manager and your cousin Barbie's brother-in-law, would get on with a fifth of whiskey, a box of tiny little Dixie cups, and a jug of water. Each member would start the day with a shot of whiskey and water!
>
> We would march in three parades that day: early morning, early afternoon (the big parade with high school bands, military units, etc.) and early evening. Then we'd play a concert at night.
>
> The thing is, before every parade when we were lining up and getting ready to start, Mike would give this command I'd never heard before. Mike would yell out, 'Powder up!'
>
> To understand that command, you have to realize that there were a lot of very old guys in the band and we were going to be marching over some primitive roads. And you should also know that the Blue Coat uniforms (which were tailored by conductor Ralph Gaspare's* father, Victor, and his Uncle Louie in 100% worsted wool) had a special pocket sewn into the skirt of the jacket.

---

*This Ralph Gaspare is the grandson of Professor Ralph Gaspare mentioned a few chapters ago who was also a tailor. In the family tradition, the Professor's sons, Victor and Louie were expert musicians.

This was where all the guys with false teeth carried their denture powder. And at the 'Powder up!' command, they took out their powder and they took out their teeth and then, well, they powdered up. I'm not saying there were a lot of them, but it looked like a snow storm.

Most of these guys were brass players. Victor Gaspare, besides being their tailor, was also their teacher. He had taught them to play with minimal pressure because of their false teeth.

By the way, the band didn't always take a bus to Follansbee. They originally drove several cars. But they switched over to the Smeal Bus Company when they began to worry about highway mayhem due to exhaustion and/or drunkenness. This put quite a crimp in some members' plans as they had no wheels to drive to nearby Steubenville between parades, either to get laid—Steubenville had quite a reputation—or to visit the birthplace of Dean Martin."

36
THE PECKHORN

In Emma Scogna Rocco's book, *Italian Wind Bands*, she describes the instrumental make-up of your average Italian band as having a horn section. And yet, if you look at the pictures of those old bands throughout her book, you won't see any French horns. The reason is, there weren't any. What was used instead of the French horn was the E-flat alto horn, or as we called them for reasons I don't know, peckhorns. We also derogatorily called them "rain catchers" due to the direction of their bell, which faced up. They look like small baritone horns, have a rather thin sound and most of the peckhorn players I remember seemed to always have a very wide vibrato.

The French horn players who joined the Italian bands in more recent years, at least the ones I knew, all seemed to have a disdain for the peckhorns. You should understand that French hornists are an arrogant breed to begin with, and the peckhorns gave them an easy target. But the instrument, easier to play than a French horn, allowed many not-so-talented but very loyal musicians to join those Italian bands. And if it weren't for the peckhorns in those bands, many an "oom" would have had no "pa-pa."

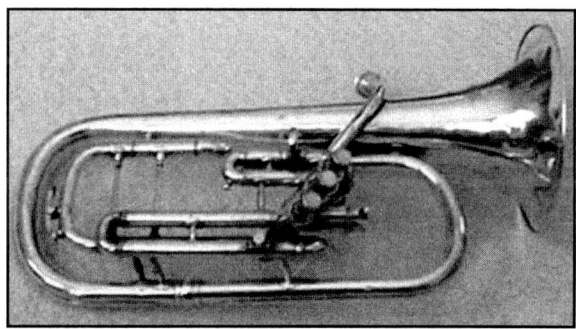

This Holton alto horn was recently up for auction on eBay.

37
MY SHORT LIFE AS A PROFESSIONAL MUSICIAN

The summer I played with the Red Coat Band, I joined the musicians' union. Had to, or I couldn't play with them. Mike Isabella, a trombonist and local bar owner, was the New Castle union president in those days. (His bar had a picture of him next to James Petrillo, the head of the national union, and for whom Chicago's Petrillo Band Shell was named.) All my cousin clarinetists belonged to the union. My French horn playing brother-in-law too. Joining was like a rite of passage, and my parents were very proud.

Financially speaking, my joining the union was stupid. As it turned out, I didn't play many paying jobs. When the Red Coats' conductor, Bebe Biondi, contracted for a job, it was usually for a certain number of players. For them to use me usually meant that somebody else didn't get to play, maybe an 80-year-old clarinetist with arthritic fingers, or a peckhorn player who would fall asleep any time he had more than a measure of rests. Chances were good that those two guys were Republicans and I wasn't even old enough to vote yet. And I'm sure Bebe thought a bassoon was a luxury that you couldn't even hear most of the time, which I have to admit was true in that band. As a result, my total earnings as a professional musician, minus union dues and other charges came to about $30 for the entire summer.

On the other hand, the union meetings were an eye-opening lesson in reality. Up to then, I took the word "play," as in "play your clarinet," literally. I thought people "played" music for the fun of it. *I* certainly did. But at these meetings, I saw for the first time that music wasn't all fun and games. Musicians, it turned out, took music seriously. Their families actually depended on the money they made teaching and playing. It provided a significant portion of their income.

So instead of the friendly chit-chat of musicians discussing the relative merits of Rossini and Verdi that I expected, the union meetings were filled with territorial disputes, with anger and hostility, with the whining and bitching of jealous and insecure egos. Rights had to be protected. Turf had to be defended. This was the one place where mediocre musicians didn't have to take a second seat to anybody. Everybody paid the same dues, so everybody had equal shouting rights. There was a lot of equal shouting.

That summer, the big problem for union musicians was the electric organ. More and more of New Castle's bars were replacing their weekend combos with organists who could play the same music as the bands, but at a fraction of the cost, since there was only one organist. If this went on, for every musician working a weekend gig, three or four would be sitting home. The arguments and flaring tempers over this fact of life seemed petty to me at first, but little by little I began to understand the passions of working people who fought so hard to protect their livelihood.

As big as the organ problem was, it was eventually overshadowed by the invasion of rock & roll bands. Non-union rock groups, mere teenagers who couldn't play their way out of a paper bag, were taking more and more jobs away from the real musicians. There were two reasons. First, the world was falling in love with rock & roll, which was bad music to the ears of these guys and they'd never catch on to it. And second, the young rock groups played for next to nothing, the dummies.

These meetings were such an education I kept on attending them even after the summer and my professional career were over. I learned three valuable lessons at those meetings that I've used all my life:

1. People feel threatened by other people's success.
2. Never count on the status quo to stick around forever.
3. Never turn your back on an electric organist.

38
MR. PETRILLO

James Caesar Petrillo, a trumpet player from Chicago, was the president of the American Federation of Musicians from 1940 to 1958. During his 18 years in office, he was a favorite target of comedians, pundits and editorial cartoonists, probably because he had this weird idea that musicians should be paid for their work. He dared to call a nationwide musicians' strike soon after the United States got into World War II. It lasted 27 months despite President Roosevelt's protest that music was essential to national wartime moral. In the end, though, Petrillo won.

What he won was living wages and job security for musicians, as well as a fairer share of the profits of the fast-growing recording industry. Until then, musicians were paid by whim, could be fired as soon as someone cheaper came along, and received no royalties on record sales.

His victory also led to the establishment of the Music Performance Trust Fund. A small percentage of the price of every record sold went into this fund and it was used to pay musicians to play free concerts all over the country. (I think the little money I made during my summer as a professional musician came from this fund.)

So the next time you enjoy a free concert in the park by professional musicians, chances are pretty good that you have Mr. Petrillo to thank.

From Eventful Decade, a book of anti-Petrillo cartoons collected and republished by the American Federation of Musicians around 1950

39
THE MUSICIAN'S SUIT

In New Castle, when a musician came of age he went out and bought himself a navy blue suit, a musician's suit.

The reason he did was because the dance bands in town were somewhat interchangeable. Rarely did a band have permanent members and a name, like "The 5 Whatevers."

If you were having a wedding or a party and wanted to hire a band, you'd call "Somebody You Knew." In New Castle, you never spent any significant money without first checking out "Somebody You Knew." Sometimes, if you didn't have "Somebody You Knew" yourself, you'd have to call "Somebody Who Knew a Guy." Eventually, you'd reach somebody like Al DeVivo and ask him if he could get a band for you. If Al wasn't already booked for the night when you needed a band, he'd settle on a price with you and then start calling around to see who was available. He had his list of favorites, of course, but rarely were they all free. So Al would go down the list and eventually form a band of musicians who weren't already booked or on a fishing trip that day.

So then, for your wedding or party, you'd have "The Al DeVivo Band" and they'd all be wearing the same navy blue musician's suit, just like a real dance band.

I never had the need for a musician's suit.

40
SANTY CLAUS

New Castle had its fair share of oddballs, characters and otherwise special people. There was Crazy Mary who always carried the same mysterious package with her wherever she went. And she kept wrapping and unwrapping it, over and over again, for years. Running Jim, as you might guess by the name, never walked, always ran. Johnny Meow would stiffen the fingers of both hands into claws and leap out at people and yell, "Meow!"

And there was the Green Man who lived outside of town a ways. He had been struck by lightning and was not only green but had no nose, lips or ears. High school kids looking for excitement would pile into their father's cars and go on late-night excursions to see if they could sneak up to his house and catch sight of him. Then, if they actually saw him, they'd run away as fast as they could so he wouldn't catch them and rip them to shreds. (I never went on one of those trips myself. When I found out that he was actually a pretty nice guy and not that scary, I lost interest.)

My favorite was Santy Claus, who's real name was Jimmy Clause. He wasn't called Santy Claus because he looked like the jolly old elf—he had no facial hair, nor did he have a big belly that shook when he laughed. He was called Santy Claus partially because of his last name, of course. But mostly because when he told you he was Santa Claus, he could be very convincing.

You see, Jimmy—a gentle, always smiling, personable soul who loved kids, parades, bands and funerals—had a very special talent for lying. He was a great impostor.

There were times when he was Santa Claus, especially for young children. But at other times, he was a surgeon. Or an army officer. Or whoever the situation called for. In all of his roles, not just for the little kids, but for adults too, he was very, very believable.

There's the story that during WWII, he rushed into a hotel in Philadelphia late at night, dressed as an Army colonel. He announced to the hotel's staff that the 2nd Army was coming through town in a few hours and they needed the hotel for their headquarters! The hotel evacuated all the guests to make room.

Another time, "Colonel" Clause went into a radio station and ordered them to cease operations due to urgent military needs. They believed him too.

Jimmy actually did enlist in the Army. It's amazing that the local draft board didn't know who, or what, they were signing up. And it's also amazing that it took the Army a few months to discover his "specialness" and discharge him. But Jimmy was very proud of the short time he spent serving his country and often wore his colonel's uniform at public functions. (You read right. Somehow, somewhere, he had managed to get himself a real U.S. Army colonel's uniform.)

Back at the home front, there was the time that Jimmy phoned Louie Prima's agent*, negotiated a date and price, and hired Prima's band to play for a dance at Cascade Park. When the agent had a small question regarding the contract, he contacted BeBe Biondi, who at that time was in charge of hiring all the bands at Cascade. BeBe of course, didn't know what the agent was talking about.

I never knew Jimmy's real name until years after I left New Castle. To me and everybody in town, he was known as Santy Claus. And everybody in town really did know him. He attended just about every funeral there was. He jauntily marched alongside the Red Coat or Blue Coat band during all the parades while dressed in his colonel's uniform, of course, and strangers probably thought he was the band leader. In fact, he was occasionally invited to conduct a march during concerts. Which he did proudly and very well.

---

*It could have been Tommy Dorsey's agent. Or Glenn Miller's. The band changes with the person telling the story. By the way, did you know that Louie Prima wrote the song *Sing, Sing, Sing* that Benny Goodman made famous?

I had my own experience with Santy Claus's credibility. One night while I was packing up my bassoon after a concert in New Castle, he wandered onto the stage, as if he belonged there, and approached me, smiling. He said he really admired me because I played a very difficult instrument but one of the orchestra's most beautiful. And he went on to describe one of his favorite passages, the bassoon quartet in Verdi's *Requiem* that he first heard while playing violin under Toscanini. He even hummed a few bars, which I recognized because I had played the *Requiem* at school a few months earlier. If I hadn't known better. . .

41
BAND OF ANGLOS

The New Castle American Legion Band was very different from other bands in New Castle, mainly because its membership contained no relatives of mine. In fact, most of its members didn't even have Italian last names. I had no idea who they were or where they came from (although I suspect it had something to do with World War II).

There were three reasons why the "establishment" musicians in town, most of whom were Italian, didn't play in it: (1) it didn't pay; (2) jobs that *did* pay, plus teaching, kept them pretty busy and their wives said enough is enough; and (3) they hated to march. So the members of the American Legion Band tended to be younger, unmarried guys with names like Lewis or Harris, and they weren't good enough to play for pay. There were a few exceptions—Frank Zaccarelli for instance was not only Italian, he played trumpet as well as anybody in town—but it was generally a rag-tag bunch of kids, vets and musical misfits.

But that changed in the early 50's when my brother-in-law Ken Meine became the conductor of the band. Ken was a stranger, a newcomer to New Castle, but he was such a fantastic French horn player, he soon became highly respected by the musicians in town in spite of the fact that he was non-Italian and pretty skinny. He brought his love of Richard Strauss and Wagner and other great non-Italian composers to New Castle, and many musicians found him refreshing. It didn't hurt that he had a personality that was very simpatico with many of them, i.e., he liked to drink, eat, and tell jokes. Whatever the reason, when he became the conductor, the American Legion Band got a face-lift.

While many of the town's best musicians still didn't have the time to become Legion Band regulars, they did send their best students. And occasionally, when they didn't have jobs to play or wives to obey (and when marching wasn't involved), they showed up themselves, just for the fun of it. And when everybody came, mostly for rehearsals, but sometimes for a concert, it was a great band.

There was Johnnie Bonfield at trumpet who taught many of the good trumpet players in town, and eventually took over as conductor of the Red Coat Band. Roger Pecano on clarinet was so quiet, but played so beautifully and reminded me of Benny Goodman. And Al DeVivo was there lots of times, too, on clarinet or flute. The horn section may have been the best horn section in the country outside of a major symphony orchestra, with my brother-in-law's three very accomplished students, Alan Zollar, Joe Hahn and Kent Malley. There was Harry Beckmeyer who played a hell of a baritone horn (and could drink more beer than anybody I'd ever met). Mike Isabella made such a big trombone sound that, while he may have lacked some finesse, he could become a whole trombone section all by himself. Mike Ferraro on flute came down from nearby Bessemer where he was the high school band director. I'll never forget the first night he joined us and played that marvelous duet with the oboe in the middle of the *William Tell Overture*. The band applauded him. They had never heard it done correctly before.

And of course, what other American Legion band had such a stellar bassoon section as Jim Haven and me. Most American Legion bands didn't even have a bassoon section.

The American Legion band gave us what the the high school band didn't—a fun, learning, musical experience. We played music no band in New Castle had ever played before, like the overture to Richard Strauss's *Der Rosenkavalier*. But we also played stuff we had played thousands of times, like *William Tell*, or even a march like *The Stars and Stripes*. And it was as though we were playing them for the first time.

I remember our Thursday night rehearsals a lot more than I remember the performances. Every piece we practiced gave us gifts that we never knew existed. We were constantly challenged and humbled and rewarded. We swore a lot at our mistakes. But we also laughed a lot, often at those same mistakes. The important thing is that we we enjoyed making music more than we thought we would, because we played it better than we thought we could.

42
THE NIGHT WE MET THE *1812 OVERTURE*

There came an American Legion Band rehearsal when Ken introduced us to *The 1812 Overture*.

On the evening the music was handed out to the band, we were mostly high school kids. Few of us had heard the *1812*. Ken explained that it had to do with Napoleon and Russia and war and triumph and all that. When he finally gave the downbeat, all of us immediately began to fall in love with it and played it with great enthusiasm. We actually did pretty well for sight reading, and we were all getting into it, getting caught up in Tchaikovsky's heroics and grandeur.

Unfortunately, during the big finish we had no cannons, guns or fireworks. It had sounded so good up until then, but with no explosives, it sort of fizzled out like a wet firecracker. Ken stopped the band and suggested that the percussionists improvise some noise during that section.

He started us up again and when we got to the big finish for the second time, it wasn't much better. The drummers just beat their drums a little harder and it still sounded lame. He stopped us.

This time his request for a more spirited improvisation was embellished by accusations involving the percussionists' gender, ancestors and eating habits. And then he promised to use certain parts of the drummers' bodies for drumstick storage if they didn't make more sound than that. He was inspirational that way.

We started once more. This time, when the band reached the big finish, the percussionists rose to the challenge. They threw cymbals against the wall. They dropped chimes on the floor. They kicked over their chairs and music stands. They clobbered each other with bass drum mallets to make each other scream. They threw loose change at the xylophone and eventually overturned it. And so on.

I gotta tell you, I've played the *1812* many times since that first night. It's never sounded as good.

43
CONVENTIONAL WISDOM

197

American Legion conventions were big highlights of my life in those days. Our New Castle band went to state conventions held in Pittsburgh and Philadelphia. A bunch of us also belonged to the Salem, Ohio American Legion Band, so we went to state conventions in Columbus, Ohio, too. The Salem band also took us to the national conventions in Chicago and Miami.

When we went on these trips, the local American Legion post would pay for our travel, they'd pay our hotel and then they'd give us $15 a day for food.

Make sure you understand what this meant to me. The only time I'd ever been out of New Castle was when my parents took Janice and me to a railroad fair in Chicago when I was 8 years old. On that trip we shared two very small, very hot rooms in a hotel next to the el tracks. We stayed 3 days. We saw some old trains. We came home.

But on these convention trips, there would be no parents, no little sisters, no old trains. Instead I would be traveling with most of my best high school buddies. And there would be some pretty swinging older guys too. There would be adventure. There would be booze. There would be exotic night clubs and wild parties. And there'd be beautiful big-city women who were hungry for guys just like me.

And I was being given $15 a day to buy as much of it as possible.

Was this Heaven, or what?

44
JAMMIN' IN PHILLY

One of the best rhymes ever is in the lyrics of the opening song of the musical *1776*: "It's hot as hell, in Philadel - phia."

The first American Legion convention I ever went to was in Philadelphia. It was during the summer of 1955. And it was hot as hell. The band stayed at the St. James Hotel, a little south on Broad Street. I thought it was a pretty neat hotel at the time, but what did I know? The last hotel I stayed in had an el train running past my bedroom window.

After checking in, we were free to do anything we wanted to do until parade time the next day. Most of the older guys in the band quickly took off for good restaurants, bad bars and big parties. But us younger guys never had a chance to chase our dreams of sex, booze and adventure. The reality was that we were too young to get into any place that had any of the above. So we did the next best thing. We hung around.

But that wasn't so bad. It was a hot night. There was a convention going on with a lot old farts in town really whooping it up. Standing outside the hotel on Broad Street, we saw drunks and whores (and a few drum and bugle corps) marching in and out of hotels. We saw panhandlers. We saw Cadillac convertibles carrying chubby, bald-headed guys and beautiful women too young to be their wives. We saw stuff the likes of which we never saw in New Castle.

At some point, we decided that we wanted to take part in this summer night's celebration, too. We decided to have a jam session, right there in front of the hotel. So we all went to our rooms and got our instruments. And we came back and jammed.

I'd like to say that we sounded wonderful, and people gathered around and danced and sang and asked for more, and three beautiful girls came by and liked us so much they invited us to come and entertain at a big bash upstairs. That, of course, was our intention. Unfortunately, we didn't sound wonderful, we sounded terrible. While we were all pretty good at reading music, none of us could fake worth a damn. So nobody gathered round. And nobody sang and danced.

But we did get one request. To leave.

A cop car pulled up and a very big policeman got out and came over to us and, of all things, he smiled very friendly like. He apologized for interrupting our music, but there had been complaints from somebody inside the hotel. He told us that he felt bad about that, since it seemed like we were just having fun and weren't causing any trouble. And then he suggested that we go to the hotel up the street a block and play for them a while. And then, when they complained up there, we could come back to the Saint James and try again.

What a nice cop. We thanked him and considered it. But instead we put our instruments away. And went back to hanging around.

45
MARCHING TO DIFFERENT DRUMMERS

We had a band crisis that summer when we went to Philadelphia. Due to sickness, defection, paying gigs and other reasons, we came up short on snare drummers. We didn't have a single one and we were desperate. We couldn't go to the convention without snare drummers!

Most of the other bands and the drum and bugle outfits would have about a thousand drummers each, and if we wanted to march, let alone win any parade prize money, we needed drummers. Lots of them.

Ken came through. Somehow, he managed to talk his old friend Jim Wisler into joining the band. Jim, a former member of the Marine Band and the author of books on drum method, was teaching percussion at Youngstown College (now Youngstown State University), 20 miles away. He not only decided to join us, he brought a couple of students with him. Dale Rauschenberg and Joe Parlink. Man, those guys were good!

When we got to Philadelphia, Jim and his two students were our snare drum section. You'd think, with only three of them, they'd get lost in the echos of all those other snare drummers in the parade, but you'd be wrong. Because, before the parade, Jim handed Dale and Joe these special drumsticks to use. They had ends that were about the size and shape of golf balls.* They weren't drumsticks, they were weapons! As a result, their rat-a-tats became RAT-A-GODDAM-TAT! And they sounded like a dozen drummers!

It wasn't only the bigger bangs of our three drummers that were so impressive. The best part was their playing. It was pure artistry. They turned "street beats," the usually mundane drumming patterns that are played between the marches in a parade, into a virtuoso performance.

Their patterns were so precise and so intricate! And they kept changing them,

---

*You often see drumsticks like these in today's marching groups, especially with drum and bugle corps, but back then they were new.

never repeating a single one, switching from 4/4 to 6/8 and back just for the fun of it. I had never heard drummers like them before or since, even with some of the great drum and bugle corps groups I've heard over the years.

If it's possible to march like a military band on the outside, but strut like a New Orleans funeral jazz band on the inside, that's what our band was doing that summer day in Philadelphia. We couldn't wait to finish *Colonel Bogey* or *Washington Post* or whatever, so we could swing through the streets of Philly, marching along to Wisler's drummers pounding out those wonderful street beats.

And our band won a first prize in the parade.

46
JOE HAHN

I met Joe Hahn when I joined the American Legion Band.

He was one of the most dedicated musicians I knew. And one of the least ambitious people I knew. He had a degree in musicology and did some composing and arranging. He played French horn with some bands and did a few combo gigs on string bass. And he occasionally directed church choirs. But he didn't get paid much for any of that, and he never held on to a steady job. I don't think he wanted one. He bartended for Mike Isabella for a while. Taught school for a while.

But mainly he read, practiced, and took care of his huge collections of jazz records, science fiction books and old radio shows.

Joe became a family member. He took horn lessons from Ken and spent a lot of time out at the greenhouse. He did a lot of baby-sitting for Ev's and Ken's four boys. Although he was a few years older than me, we hung around together quite a bit. We shared interests in science fiction, movies and not doing anything strenuous.

Joe was the one who taught me how to be cool.

He taught me the difference between hip and hep. At that time, hip was hip, but hep was passé.

He taught me how to use the words "man," "like," and "dig" to maximum effect. I got so good at it that when I went to college, I was able to carry on the following conversation with a friend in the band:

ME: Hey man, did you dig that new flick yet?

PAL: Yeah, man. I dug it last night, but like, I didn't dig it, you dig?

ME: I dig.*

---
*Translation:
ME: I say, old chap, by any chance did you happen to see the new offering at the cinema yet?
PAL: Yes, my friend, I did. But to tell you the truth, it wasn't my cup of tea, if you get my meaning.
ME: Say no more. I completely understand.

Joe taught me that my clarinet was my "ax" and so was my bassoon.

He taught me that "bad" was good, "terrible" was great, "horrible" was even better, but "the worst" was, in fact, the worst. Usually.

And he told me that real musicians never carry their ax case by the handle. It wasn't cool. Instead you carry it under your arm, which was cool when my ax was the clarinet. But it wasn't so cool with that big bassoon case. You dig?

Joe died a couple of years ago, too early. He left behind a book he'd been writing for years. It was an encyclopedia of every instance of science fiction that occurred on television since its beginning. Every single one! He had catalogued every *Captain Video and the Video Rangers*, every *I Dream of Jeannie*, every instance of time travel, rocketry, robotics, alien invasion, and much, much more. About a year before he died, he sent it to me, asking for ideas about what he could do with it when it was finished. For the life of me, I couldn't come up with a single suggestion. Hell, I couldn't get past the first few pages, and I love science fiction.

Joe was a good musician, a good friend, a gentle man, and he should be remembered. That's why, if you walk along Lake Michigan in Gilson Park in Wilmette, Illinois, you'll pass a flowering apple tree with a plaque underneath that says, "In memory of Joe Hahn."

47
SWIMMING POOLS, SAUSAGE AND WOODWIND QUINTETS

Evelyn and Ken lived a few miles south of New Castle on Savannah Road. They owned greenhouses there. Ken grew flowers for wholesale, mostly snapdragons and carnations. They had a big old house on the side of a hill about half a mile from the road.

One summer we built a swimming pool next to the house with a huge cement patio to go with it. The pool was fed by an underground stream of the coldest water known to man, so we actually did very little swimming there.

The view from the patio was of vast cornfields owned by Weinschenk's, a big veggie grower and seller in the area. As scenery, you wouldn't buy the post card, but as an after-dinner treat, it was delicious. Many's the summer night we put on dark clothes, greased up our faces and made forays in those fields to capture the elusive corn on the cob. We weren't greedy. We only took what we could eat.

Since Ken was the conductor of the American Legion Band, he and Ev thought it would be a nice treat to have a combination band rehearsal and picnic on the patio. It was a perfect summer day. Band members brought their wives. Friends and family showed up. And a few young and stupid guys, probably trumpet players, actually went swimming in the cold water.

We had Italian sausage sandwiches—your choice of hot and mild, with the sausage slathered in spaghetti sauce and sprinkled with Parmesan cheese. There was probably a lot of other stuff to eat, but I can only remember the sausage. For drink, there was lots of red wine (was there such a thing as *white* wine in those days?), cases of Iron City Beer and lots of non-diet pop, probably because diet pop wasn't invented yet.

Before the rehearsal, Anita, who had shown up with her oboe, brought out some woodwind quintet music. While everybody was outside putting away huge amounts of the sausage, a few of us went inside the house and did the quintet thing. Anita was on oboe, Roger Pecano played clarinet, Joe Hahn was on horn and Mike Ferraro played flute. And since Jim Haven was out of town that day, I got the bassoon part all to myself. It was the first time I had played woodwind quintet music, and I can't tell you how much I enjoyed it. It was wonderful.

But the thing I learned about woodwind quintets that day is there's no way an audience can enjoy them a fraction as much as the players do. I realized that I would hate to hear anyone have so much fun without me. So, to this day, I've never gone to a woodwind quintet concert. Great to play in. Boring to sit through.

But the band rehearsal was the high point. We were a really good band that day because most of our best musicians had shown up. It was early evening when we started, warm but with a refreshing, soft wind. We had set up the seats and music stands on the patio and when we played, our notes grabbed onto the breeze and rolled over the countryside. The one piece I remember playing was the overture to *Die Meistersinger* which seemed very appropriate for the setting. Maybe a little Wagnerian thunder and lightning would have made it even better, but we made do. Cars stopped and parked all along Savannah Road to listen to us.

There's a thing that happens sometimes in band and orchestra rehearsals but not very often. It's when all the counting, reeds, clefs, beats, rhythms, key signatures, sharps, flats, fingerings and so on all disappear and the music takes over. It's when everybody gets it exactly right, all at the same time. You get into a groove, and you are all doing something together that's so beautiful and so perfect, you want to cry for the joy of it. That's what it felt like for me that day.

Of course, I had consumed quite a bit of the wine before we started.

48
THE AUDITION

There came a time when I realized that I was a high school senior and I was going to graduate real soon. While most of my friends already knew which colleges they were going to, I had been having too much fun in bands, in plays, in student council, in socializing to worry about the future.

I had given no thought to what I wanted to be when I grew up. All I could think about were the things I *didn't* want to be, i.e., doctor, lawyer, engineer, teacher, scientist, businessman or anything else. Sure, music was fun, but I was beginning to realize that I would never get rich as a musician.

The other problem was money. Although my parents eventually footed the bill for my college education—I was, after all, "The Son"*—at that time they weren't making me any offers. As far as I knew, I was going to have to pay my own way.

To sum up, I didn't know where I was going, what I was going to study, or how I was going to pay for it. But time was running out and a decision had to be made. So I decided to use my BTC (Bassoon Trump Card).

It was my belief that bassoonists were so rare that any college with a music school would be glad to offer a scholarship to a nice, semi-talented kid like me who had studied with a member of a major symphony orchestra. Once enrolled, I could switch from music into a major that was closer to what I really wanted to study, whatever that turned out to be. And because good bassoonists were so hard to come by, I might even be able to keep the scholarship, just to fill the seat in their orchestra. Not a bad plan, right? I settled on the Cincinnati Conservatory of Music as the place where I might carry out my scheme. Not only was it a good school but, more important, it was the only university still accepting applica-

---

*My sisters to this day maintain that I was spoiled rotten as a kid and had the benefit of many privileges that they didn't enjoy, because I was "The Son." My reaction to this is, "So? What's your point?"

tions. They were going to hold auditions for the music school in Canton, Ohio, in two weeks.

For my audition piece, I chose a bassoon concerto, I think it was a Weber. And man did I practice. It was the hardest and longest I ever practiced for anything. Janice was my accompanist and every night, after dinner, we'd sit at the piano and play until my lip gave out. I remember it was difficult. I remember wishing I had Ben Spiegel to help me. I remember my mother yelling for us to do the dishes. But by the time of the audition, I knew that piece cold. Damn, I was good!

On the Sunday of the audition, Janice and I got into the Studebaker and drove to Canton, about a 90-mile trip. We arrived at the address of the church where the auditions were being held with about 15 minutes to spare. I quickly stuck my favorite reed into my mouth to get it wet and warm, and we hurried in.

There was this one little problem. No auditions were being held there that day. Or any other day as far as the janitor knew.

The janitor was the only person there.

We looked around. We listened for music. We checked directions. We checked the map. Nothing.

So we did the only thing we could. We got into the car and drove back to New Castle.

You may not believe this, but we laughed all the way home.

You probably think I screwed up somewhere along the line and got the directions wrong.

But at that time, and still today, I figured it was God telling me to quit messing around and get a life. If so, it worked. From that day on, I stopped thinking of myself as a musician, or even as a potential musician, and discovered that there were a lot of other things to do, too.

49
THE AGE OF INNOCENTS

I graduated high school in 1956. (You remember "The Chicks of '56" don't you?) It was during that small, peaceful island of time between Korea and Viet Nam when boys wore buckles on the butts of their pants and had just started to grow their crew cuts into DA's. Girls still wore skirts instead of pants to school, and they hadn't turned their hair into beehives yet.

I was one of what Calvin Trillin calls "The Fifties Guys," who came along between the World War II Guys and the Boomer Guys. We were mainly noted for our boring lack of ill will and our blatant good manners.

We were the *Leave it to Beaver* and the *Father Knows Best* generation and not very exciting at all. Trillin wrote:

> In our defense, opportunities for disgraceful behavior were limited by circumstances beyond our control. There weren't any shooting wars to slither out of. The term recreational drugs. . .had not been coined. The sort of state lawbreaking that Fifties Guys were associated with was underage drinking. The sort of federal lawbreaking that Fifties Guys were associated with was underage drinking with a fake draft card. . .*

It was an uncomplicated time for music, too. There was no such thing as a keyboard player in those days. There were no drum machines, no synthesizers. Elvis's pelvis was just beginning to make a name for itself. The Beatles were but a gleam in Ed Sullivan's eyes. Big bands were still big. Rock was just a baby. We listened and danced cheek-to-cheek to Ralph Martieri, Stan Kenton, Woody Herman, Count Basie, Sauter & Finnegan, Les and Larry Elgart, Billy May and Benny Goodman. We loved the Hi-Lo's and the Four Freshman, especially with Pete Rugolo's seven trombones. We went to hear band concerts in the park. And there were still vets from the Civil War marching in our parades.

---

*Time magazine (9/27/99)

It may sound a bit boring by today's standards, but on the other hand, we had no wars, no drugs, no road rage, no Jerry Springer.

Okay, we had the atom bomb scare, and it was really scary, let me tell you—we were sure the world would blow itself up any day now. And I now know that there were a lot of race and class and sex and economic problems that would soon capture the attention of the whole country. But back then, I suffered the sweet bliss of stupidity.

My main goals in life were to read every science fiction book ever written, do as little physical labor as possible, memorize as many dirty jokes as I could, find a girl who would let me touch her breasts, and make music—not necessarily in that order. Life was pretty damn good.

Then all of a sudden, reality rained on my parade. I was forced to go away, into that cold, cruel world outside of New Castle, first to college where I'd probably have to actually study, and then to a job where I'd probably have to actually work.

50
YOU CAN TAKE THE BOY
OUT OF THE BAND, BUT...

While my career as a professional musician never quite got off the ground, I hadn't yet played my last note. What follows is a medley of my subsequent musical highlights.

1956 - My Country Calls

I spent my first college year at Youngstown College. I went there because it was the only school I could get into on such short notice. And I was lucky to get in. It may have helped that Anita worked in the registrar's office at the time.

Early every morning, I would ride from New Castle to Youngstown in Anita's 1949 Studebaker convertible (my family had a Studebaker gene). I had a part-time job selling women's shoes at Strouss's Department store in Youngstown. I majored in Public Relations. I took a badminton class and aced it. I took an archery class and got a bull's eye.

Because it was a "land grant" school, whatever that is, ROTC (Reserve Officers Training Corps) was mandatory at Youngstown College. I, of course, followed the family tradition and joined the ROTC band to keep out of harm's way. This protected me from the laughter of my friends, laughter that I heard every time I walked through campus in the ill-fitting, heavy wool, outdated WWII army uniform that I was forced to wear. As a member of the band, I could march through the campus with 30 other guys, all dressed just like me. There was safety and anonymity in numbers.

1957 - The Ying Yang Band

At the end of my freshman year at Youngstown, I transferred to Penn State and became a journalism major. I also joined the Penn State Blue Band and the Penn State Orchestra. My best friends were all music majors.

During my last year there, one of those friends, Bob Navarra, and I put together a band to go to the Penn State-Army game at West Point since the Blue Band wasn't going that year. As far as I knew, we were the first band that ever went to an away Penn State game that wasn't the Blue Band.

We made no big plans. We kept our membership down to 5 players and a designated driver (a freshman pledge to Bob's fraternity) so we'd all fit into one car. It was about a 6-hour drive to West Point. And for the fun of it, none of us played our usual instruments. For instance, I played bass drum. We named ourselves the Ying Yang band after Penn State's awesome second platoon (remember second platoons?) that was called the Ying Yang Gang for some reason that probably made sense back then. We even painted my drum, which we bought at a pawn shop for $5, to say "Penn State Ying Yang Band" on its drum head.

We were somewhat limited in our repertoire. We knew only one song by heart which we called, appropriately, *The One We Know*, and we played it enthusiastically, if badly. But we did get to play it on the football field as the Penn State team ran out, both at the beginning and at half time. And we played it a lot in the stands. We also played it at the parties we were invited to after the game. We played it for drinks. We played it to impress girls. We played it until we were too drunk to play it any more and then we got sick and vomited a lot. And then we got our designated driver to drive us home. It was a lot of fun.

We were surprised when we got back to campus that our fame had spread. We were invited to play at pep rallies and parties for the rest of the season.

It's many years later now. My present home is very near Ryan Stadium in Evanston, Illinois, where the Northwestern University Wildcats play their home games. Recently we were invited by our friends, Kevin and Barbara Clary, to a Northwestern-Penn State game. The Blue Band didn't come that day, but while waiting for the opening kick-off, I happened to notice a small band of about 20 musicians in the Penn State section on the other side of the field. I got out the binoculars to take a better look, and saw that there was something written on the head of the bass drum that I couldn't quite make out.

I like to think it said "Penn State Ying Yang Band."

1964 - I Get My First New Clarinet

At age 26 and after a 3-year gig in the army, I got my first real job. I was hired as a junior copywriter at Bozell and Jacobs, an ad agency in Omaha, Nebraska. $400 a month. Wow.

My first TV commercials were written there for The Yellow Pages. One of them had some opera singers singing two words, "Yellow Pages," over and over to the music of the sextet from *Lucia di Lammermoor*. Another had a cowboy singing, to the tune of *Home on the Range*, "Oh give me a book, where my fingers can look, through pages of yeller all day."

One night early in December a few of us young, single professionals were in a Dodge Street bar having some beers and we discovered that all of us had played in our high school bands. After a another round or two of beers, my friend Margot, an anesthesiologist* who had played the baritone horn in her band, suggested that it might be fun if we dusted off our instruments and went Christmas caroling. And a few beers later, we all thought that was the best idea we had ever heard, and agreed to do it.

Which we actually did! A week later we went caroling. Since I no longer had my old, well-traveled, sat-upon and much-repaired clarinet—I think my father

---

*When anybody asked Margot what she did for a living, she always replied, "I pass gas."

gave it away to one of my cousins' kids—I splurged and went out and rented a brand new black plastic clarinet at $7 a month for the occasion. We played really badly but we had a lot of fun. (Do you sense a pattern here? Remember Philadelphia? The Ying Yang Band?) I eventually bought that clarinet, still have it and still play it occasionally, mostly around Christmas.

A note for Trivial Pursuit players: The first house on our caroling route that night belonged to my friend Bill Fries who was the head art director at Bozell. A few years after I left Omaha, Bill became fairly famous as C. W. McCall, the folk hero who recorded a hit song called *Convoy* that inspired a movie of the same name starring Burt Reynolds.

1967 - A Local Hero

A few years later, when I was working at Ketchum, McLeod and Grove in Pittsburgh, Pennsylvania (the ad agency where I met Judy, my future wife) I wrote a television commercial for Iron City Beer that was inspired by a real event that happened when I was in the New Castle American Legion Band.

We were marching in a parade in Pittsburgh. It was extremely hot that day, the parade was long, the sun was beating down on us the whole way, our uniforms were wool, and our thirst grew and grew with every step. We were so thirsty that at the end of the parade, where other bands broke ranks, took off their jackets and ties and put their instruments away, we just kept on going, marching and playing until we found the nearest bar—about a block away. We never broke our ranks, never stopped playing. We just marched straight in. Then we all ordered big, cold mugs of Iron City on tap. Sure, some of us were underage, but I think the bartender saw the desperation in our eyes and realized that this was an emergency. Man, that beer tasted good.

The commercial I wrote told that story, except I changed the band to one very much like the Red Coat or Blue Coat band. I thought the Italian band's characters and marching style would be more visually interesting. But everything else was like what really happened. I had them marching through Pittsburgh on a hot day and finally marching right into a bar where they quenched their thirst the best way possible, with cold, refreshing "Irons."

Unfortunately, I had nothing to do with the casting and shooting of the commercial. My intention was to use the real Blue Coat Band as actors, and have them march over real Pittsburgh bridges, through real Pittsburgh streets. But instead, the band members turned out to be Hollywood types with lots of hair, smooth faces and not much belly. They were too "Midigun" looking to ever be mistaken for an ethnic band. They were directed to march like a college band at half-time, swinging their instruments from side to side in time to the music. And it was shot in L.A. instead of Pittsburgh. I hated it.

But the good news is that we actually went to New Castle and recorded the Blue Coat Band's version of the Iron City jingle for the sound track. Word got around that I was responsible for getting the Blue Coats' sound, if not their bodies, on television. And the band also made some extra money. So, for a short time, I was a minor hero in New Castle.

1970 - A Visit From God

I eventually moved to Chicago to take a job at the Leo Burnett Advertising Agency. My apartment was on the 8th floor of Faulkner House in Sandburg Village, about 6 blocks west of Lake Michigan. It had a great view. A big picture window faced the lake and there were many low roof tops in between.

One night, my nephew Glenn, one of Ev's sons, dropped in for a visit and while he was there, Chicago did what it likes to do occasionally—it surprised us with a sudden, violent thunderstorm full of noise you can feel and lightning that zapped all over the sky. So, naturally, I put Prokofiev's *Lieutenant Kijé* on the stereo, turned it up loud and opened the drapes all the way on the window that faced the lake. Then I got Glenn a soda and me a beer, turned off the lights and we sat back to enjoy the show.

It turned out to be a miraculous performance. It was as if God had said, "Hey, I'm going to take some time out from my busy schedule and treat these guys to a spectacular show."

Huge cracks of thunder came from behind us, in front of us and all around us. Sometimes the lightning spotlighted the lake briefly, brightly. And at other times it was the roof tops on the left, then the roof tops on the right. Then the lake again. Sometimes the lightning zapped like the sky was being ripped open. And at other times, it just glowed and pulsed. But here's the best part. Unbelievably, incredibly, all the lightning and thunder was choreographed to the music!

When the music was *pianissimo*, so was the thunder. When there was a pause in the music, there was a pause in the storm. When the music got big and exciting and very forte like Prokofiev can do, the lightning flashed with the cymbal crashes, and the thunder thundered with the tympani. And when the piece ended, the storm ended, too. Just like that.

Glenn and I were in awe. We just sat there for a moment, stunned.

And then we each spontaneously jumped to our feet and gave God a standing ovation.

I'm not kidding. This is absolutely true. Ask Glenn.

1983 - Taking the Kids Shopping

After we got married, Judy and I lived in Chicago's Near North area for a while. But, as soon as we began to beget, we moved to Wilmette, a suburb of Chicago, about 10 miles north along the lake. We settled down to a typical life of commuting to work, schools, PTA's, softball teams, scouts, and of course, piano lessons.

I loved it when my son and two daughters were taking their piano lessons. They somehow learned the trick of reading all those notes and memorizing them and they all played beautifully. I even wrote a commercial for McDonald's patterned after my daughters' recitals and how we would go out to eat at a fast food restaurant afterwards. It had to do with a little girl playing Beethoven's *Für Elise* in front of a big, scary recital audience. To keep from getting nervous she thought about going to McDonald's after the recital. Her thinking was in the form of lyrics that she sung in her mind to the *Für Elise* melody "Oh I wish I were already there, instead of here, playing this song...." It was one of my best commercials and won several awards.

All three of my kids entered piano competitions and took their share of prizes, but my most Proud Papa moment came when Judy and I took them shopping for a new piano. We went to Saphir's, a large piano store that's a lot better than its slogan ("If it sounds good to the ear, it came from Saphir").

They were very businesslike, those kids of mine. They knew the new piano would be mainly for them and they wanted it to be a good one, the right one. So with great focus and seriousness, they marched through the store, auditioning just about every piano in the place. It was quite a concert. Here was 13-year-old Joe playing Rachmaninoff's *Polichinelle* on the Steinway. There was Kate, age 10, playing Chopin's *Fantasy Impromptu* on the Mason and Hamlin. And way over there was my youngest, little 7-year-old Becky, playing a Bach fugue on the Kawai. They did Saint-Saens, Gershwin, Debussy, Mozart and more, not just little snippets of pieces, but huge chunks.

It sounded so wonderful. It was like a scene from a 40's movie musical with José Iturbi, all those grand pianos with the lids up and these three kids moving from one to the other.

I thought my chest was going to burst.

1985 - My First Bassoon

I was driving down Green Bay Road in Wilmette one Saturday in summer and saw a sign for a yard sale. I don't know why, but I pulled the car over and got out to take a look.

I saw it right away. There, on the ground, right next to a pair of rusty andirons. A bassoon! And it had a torn square of paper next to it marked "$100!" I couldn't believe it. Bassoons are so expensive that I never owned one of my own. All the ones I played in the past belonged to the school I was going to at the time.

I got it for $75.

51
MY MOST GLORIOUS MUSICAL MOMENT OF ALL TIME!

A few months after we moved to Wilmette, we invited my family to spend Christmas with us in our new house. First my mother and father came from Pennsylvania and stayed with Judy, me and the three kids. By Christmas Eve, my three sisters, two nieces and four nephews had also joined us. The house was big and we had a long dinner table, thank God.

As you might imagine, there was a lot of preparation for this event. Judy's part was to clean the house from top to bottom, put up a few thousand Christmas decorations, bake a ton of cookies and cook a freezer full of food, plus do all the gift shopping and wrapping. My job was to order the wine. And I had one other thing to do—practice the clarinet.

I had made up my mind that after years of listening to Louie Colella, Tommy Naples and many others play Weber's *Concertino for Clarinet* at one saint's day celebration or another, now it was my turn. I was finally going to perform the *Concertino*. I would play it for my family on Christmas Eve. So I practiced and practiced. Judy took time out from scrubbing the floors, making cookies and feeding the baby to accompany me on the piano.

Then came the big night, Christmas Eve. We hurried through dinner. It only took about three hours. (Christmas Eve dinner is "The Big Eating Event of the Year!" for my family. We do the 7-fish tradition that some Italian fish store started centuries ago as a promotion. For good luck, you have to eat seven different fishes on Christmas Eve. You have your shrimp appetizers, your fish stew, your spaghetti *agli olio*—or as we say, "oily-oilies"—with anchovies, your deep-fried smelts, your codfish salad, your perch oreganato, and something else. It's like trying to remember the Seven Dwarfs. You always forget one.)

Of course, all this fish makes you very thirsty, so that night a great deal of wine was consumed, much of it accompanied by my father's many toasts cel-

52
THE BUTTON

(A button, or "stinger" as it's sometimes called, is that one note at the end of a march that tells you it's all done. As in "duuuuuuuuh... dut!" That "dut!" is the button.)

You should know that everything in this book is true. Sort of. In Federico Fellini's *8½*, he remembered a snowfall from his boyhood that was taller than people. And he remembered women with breasts that were, well, bigger than the snowfall. I'm sure that was the truth exactly as he remembered it.

And this is all exactly how I remember it. I'm sure there are others who remember it differently, perhaps even more accurately. But who knows for sure? What's really important, I think, is that we remember it somehow.

I know there were other, non-family musicians in town who deserve mentioning, like Tommy Natale who turned down a job with Louie Prima because he didn't want to leave his family. And like Tommy Frabotta who had, as far as I was concerned, the best gig possible—playing five nights a week in the pit band for the strippers at the Park Burlesque in Youngstown. And Mickey Natale, Ray Melcer, Dom Pecano, and Jack Shepp who made lots of music in and around New Castle. And there were the ones who went away, like Bill Caiazza, a very funny man who played trombone in the orchestras for many musicals in New York. And like Dante DiThomas, Chasey DeAngelis, Ralph (Garafalo) Gari, Bill Usselton, Ralph Zona, Roger DeLillo and Lou Pagano—they found careers in Hollywood, Las Vegas, New York and elsewhere. There are many, many more.

And I know there are lots of stories about music and musicians besides my own that should not be forgotten. And about other families and celebrations and traditions. (I invite everybody who reads this book to let me know their stories. Or let me know of any mistakes or omissions I've made telling my stories. I'd love to write a sequel.)

I never got around to telling you about my lip-synching to *Bulgie the Bass* or playing Gene Kelly to Janice's Cyd Charisse in *Slaughter on 10th Avenue*. Or about all my adventures in the Salem, Ohio band and about the time I played bongos in the Catskills. Or about the many recording sessions I had while working in advertising, the brand new sax Judy surprised me with one Christmas, and a few other things. But *basta é basta*. Enough is enough. You get the idea. Through music, I've had some fun, met some people, learned some lessons and made some joyful, if not always artful, noise.

But before I hit that button, I'd like to go back to where I started.

I can't imagine a better place to grow up in than New Castle. The music. The diversity. The traditions. Not to mention the pasta and wine. What else could I wish for in my formative years?

But things change. Unfortunately, the town hasn't aged well. Johnson Bronze and even Shenango Pottery are gone. The Pennsy railroad doesn't hold up traffic on Montgomery Avenue like it used to. The fires in the furnaces of the steel mills in Youngstown and Pittsburgh have gone out and a lot of jobs for New Castle men and women went with them. Too many young people have had to leave town and earn their daily bread elsewhere.

Thank God, the bands and the feasts and the fireworks are still there.

I hope that somebody reading this book will fall in love with the town, move there and open up a huge factory or two so kids won't have to move away when they grow up.

I'd like a guarantee that the bands will play for all the saints' days and celebrations forever.

Dut!

ACKNOWLEDGEMENTS (DRUM ROLL PLEASE!)

Jane Campbell, the first non-Italian descendant to read the early draft of BANDS! not only provided some important editing, but amazingly, related to everything and laughed in all the right places, sometimes hysterically. My sister Anita DeVivo, who literally wrote the book on editing, suggested many corrections but insisted on none. Evelyn Meine, Ralph Lombardo and Johnny DeAngelis provided material that I couldn't do without. It was Mike Malatak who said I should write this book in the first place. My sister Janice Aubrey accompanied me when nobody else would (okay, this doesn't have much to do with the book, but I may never get another chance to thank her in public). My daughter Kate DeVivo, with her trusty computer, helped with designs and edits and finally got me to the publisher. My wife Judy had the job of reading the first, second, third and so on drafts of every chapter, correcting all my spelling and grammar mistakes, of which there were many, and convincing me over and over again that I was doing good—for which, among many other reasons, I love her (but I'm not going to let her see this sentence as she would probably suggest that perhaps it's a bit too convoluted, and does go on and on.) And finally, there are my mother and father, Helen and Joe DeVivo, who gave me a storybook beginning.

About The Figurines

I don't know why I started to collect them. Perhaps, subconsciously, I was trying to hold on to my musical past. Or maybe it was to honor a life I couldn't lead. Or maybe I was simply bored with the endless flea markets and antique malls my wife dragged me to on weekends, so I bought a few things just to keep awake.

Whatever the reason, I've been gathering bands and musicians for years and, as my wife will tell you, the collection has grown to be embarrassingly large and quite out of control. Soon, no doubt, something will have to be done about it.

In the meantime, here's some information about the ones I've shown in this book, or as much information my faulty memory and lazy record-keeping allows. But I'll never forget the three pigs pictured on this page. They started it all, the swine.

cover   *Italian Band.* Ceramic, 5" tall, marked "Italian 8." The bassoonist is me as I appeared in my high school annual. As you can see, I was only 6" tall in those days.

pg. v   *Kewpie Doll with Bass Drum.* 3½" tall, bisque. Kewpie dolls (named after Cupid) were an invention of Rose O'Neil who wrote children's poems for the *Ladies' Home Journal* in 1909. Her cartoon drawings illustrated her writings, evolved into paper dolls, then into blue-winged dolls like mine. Even though this one is numbered, I'm pretty sure it's not one of the originals. It didn't cost enough.

vi   *Little Clown Cymbalist.* Bisque, only 2" tall, bought from Heritage Trail in Wilmette, Illinois.

ix   *Sitting Clarinetist.* There's also a sitting flautist to go with him. The pair are ceramic, 4½" tall and come from Leonard's Antique Mall on the outskirts of Beaver Falls, Pa., just south of New Castle. It's a really good antique mall if you're ever in the area.

1   *Clarinetist with Green Hat.* 4½" tall, chalk, Hull-like.

5   *Village Band.* The five pieces all look like they're playing in the same town square, but the band comes from two different countries. The string bass, snare drum and tuba players are marked "Made in Occupied Japan." I bought them on eBay from Robert Harvey. The other two musicians are marked "Germany" and are numbered. I found them at the Sandwich, Illinois flea market.

13   *Piano Player.* Ceramic, about 5" tall. He was bought at the Kane County Flea Market in St. Charles, Illinois, and came with his own stage. The flowers are plastic ones that I added (he seemed to need them). And I think there's a female singer that's supposed to go along with him. If anybody finds her, let me know.

17   *Horn Player.* 3½" tall, ceramic, marked "Japan." He has a drummer partner who looks just as goofy as he does.

21   *Pagliacci Clown.* 10½" tall, chalk. I think he's supposed to be Enrico Caruso who often starred in the title role of the opera about a clown with marital problems. I found him in an antique store in Richmond, Illinois while traveling north to visit my nephew Glenn at his blues bar in Delavan, Wisconsin.

25   *Clarinetist.* Czechoslovakian, glass. 7½" tall. Bought from Mark Shimkus on eBay.

29   *Li'l Abner and Family.* I bought this mechanical tin toy in Lebanon, Ohio while visiting my nephew Kenny and his wife Debbie in Dayton. The piano is 5½" tall.

35   *Opera Singer.* She's 5" tall and, I think, made of chalk.

39   *Barefoot Clarinet Player.* 3½" tall, ceramic except for his hair which is, well, hairy. He's part of a trio I bought from Helen Harris on eBay, labeled "Enesco, Japan."

45   *Piano Bank.* 6" tall, plastic, bought in an antique mall in St. Charles, Illinois for $2. Marked "Made in China."

51   *Jazz Quintet.* My mother and father bought this wonderful chalk quintet for $12 from Gene Scala's shop in Ellwood City, Pa. (Gene has done some wonderful, world-class glass etching in New Castle.) Then they gave it to my sister Janice instead of me! A few years ago, Janice finally consented to lend the band to me. But if she thinks she's getting it back, she's crazy. The clarinet figure is 8" tall.

57   *Deco Musicians.* Wood, about 9½" tall. I found these musicians in two different places. You can tell which are which by their bases. The black base

musicians came from John Ralston on eBay. The others came from the Broadway Antique Mall in Chicago.

63 *Frog Bassoonist.* Pewter, 1½" tall, marked "Hudson Pewter" and numbered. I've had him so long I can't remember where I got him.

67 *Turbaned Bassoonist.* Ceramic, 4" tall. This guy is a member of a 4-piece band bought at a Chicago toy store that's now out of business.

71 *Girl Bassoonist.* 4" tall, wooden, by Anri.

75 *German Soldier Bassoonist.* He's 3" tall and part of an 8-piece band marked "Elastolin Germany." I bought him from Tony Grecco on eBay.

79 *Mexican Clarinetist.* 3½" tall, ceramic, part of a delightful 10-piece band I bought from Luciano Ramirez on eBay. The figures were so unique, several people were bidding on them and it was a hard-fought battle—one of those down-to-the wire auctions that I finally won with a bid made just five seconds before the auction closed. Phew! Unfortunately, about a year later, on a trip to the Southwest, we crossed over the border to visit Nogales, Mexico, and saw hundreds of the same or similar bands for sale in tourist stores. Cheap.

83 *Crammed Symphony.* Made from some sort of composition material and only 3" tall. It's actually a tiny box bought from the *Music Stand* catalogue. If you look closely, it's hilarious. The cymbalist is banging the head of the person in front of him who appears to have a dog at his feet. And on the other side (not shown) you can see that the conductor is poking his baton into the eye of a violinist.

87 *Four Monks and an Organ.* I found this ceramic group at the same antique store in Richmond, Illinois where I found the Pagliacci clown. Obviously, it was a good day for antiquing. The monks are 5½" tall.

91   *Boston Bull Bassoonist.* One of a 6-piece band labeled "Made in Japan." Ceramic, 3¼" tall.

95   *Wacko Dog Guitarist.* A souvenir from a trip to London from my daughter, Becky. It's 4½" tall, metal and marked "Rex Sculpture, Apple Gardens, Covent Gardens."

99   *Singer.* 4½" tall, porcelain, marked "Made in Japan." This is one of a pair. The other one is a violinist.

103 *Three Marchers.* Russian, bought from Arkady Reznikov at Russian Antiquity. They're ceramic and 2¼" tall.

107 *Big Mouth Operatic Quartet.* 5" tall and the label says "1986, S.J. Anderson." I espied (always wanted to use that word) them in the window of a music store while driving along Chicago Avenue in Evanston, Illinois (I had keen eyes back then). I immediately pulled over, double parked and ran in and bought them. Made from some composition, I think.

113 *Tiny Symphony.* About 1" tall, lead, bought from the *Lilliputian* catalogue.

117 *Bass Drummer Planters.* I didn't get these two at the same place. The boy was bought at Leonard's Antique Mall. I can't remember where I got the girl. They're ceramic, 6½" tall and have no marks.

121 *Majorettes with Music Notes.* 4" tall, ceramic not counting the feathers. They're marked "Japan" in red. I like to think of them as Sandy Wochner, Adrienne Lloyd, Natalie Colecchi and Barbara Dunlop who were our majorettes at Ne-Ca-Hi. (Not pictured are the ones I like to think of as Francis Parenti, Judy Bender, Barbara Waddington, Nancy Logan, Floreen Colella, Gracie Cook, Sandy DeRosa and Judy Vago.)

125 *Band with Shako Hats.* Cardboard, on wooden bases, 6½" tall, bought through a mail auction.

131 Soldier Trio. Lead, 2" tall not counting the flag.

135 Red-Coated Band. Lead Britains with movable arms, 2¼" tall, bought in Glenview, Illinois.

141 Girl with Tambourine. 5" tall, plastic, marked "Hong Kong," bought on a car trip to visit our son in Atlanta.

147 Veggie and Fruit Quartet. About 4" tall, ceramic salt and pepper shakers. The cucumber and banana on the left were bought from Dallas Kinkead on eBay and labeled "National Potteries Co., Cleveland, Ohio." I can't remember where I got the other two. All four are marked "Napco, Japan."

151 12-Piece Orchestra. 2" tall, wood, "Made in Japan." The cardboard box is marked "Canibal."

155 String Players. 11" tall, metal, bought at a roadside stand along Route I-95, in North Carolina, I think.

161 Blue-Coated Band. 2½" tall, bisque. The label says "Made exclusively for Lemax. Made in China."

165 Strange Peckhorn Player Toothpick Holder. A strange accordion player and strange string bass player go with him. All three are bisque, 4½" tall, marked "Paulux Made in Japan."

169 Mechanical Piano Player. Mostly plastic, battery driven. About 7" tall, marked "Made in China." He moves side to side as he plays. Bought at Chicago's North Pier area the summer my daughter Becky worked there.

173 Dog Trumpet Player. 5" tall, bisque, marked "Made in China." He's one of a four-piece band I bought from Jan Biven on eBay.

177 Deco Jazz Quartet. 3" tall, ceramic, bought in Los Angeles. I had seen the band a year before while I was in L.A. but didn't buy them because I thought they were too expensive and, of course, regretted not buying them as soon as I left town. A year later, I went to the same antique store on Melrose, and amazingly they were still there. The price was the same, but I had gotten a raise by then.

181 *Santa Claus Trio.* 6½" tall, ceramic.

187 *WWI Soldier Band.* 2¼" tall, lead.

193 *Napoleonic Band.* 2¾" tall, lead. Bought at the Grove Street Antique Mall in New Castle, Pa. The box says "Made in Hong Kong for the Treasure Chest of Orange Park, Florida."

197 *Blue Band of Britains.* 2½" tall, lead, 1986.

201 *Swing Band.* They're not marked but I think they're chalk and made in Japan. The clarinetist is 6¾" tall.

205 *Rabbit (maybe Mouse?) Nodders.* Almost 5" tall, wood, marked "Japan."

209 *Clown French Horn Player.* 9" tall, ceramic, marked "Italy," and numbered. I also have a matching drummer. Christmas gift from Judy.

213 *Classical Quintet.* 5½" tall, bisque, labeled "Vcagco Ceramics, Japan." Gift from my sister Evelyn, who has a rather large musician collection of her own.

217 *Little Duo.* Just 1" tall, lead, and marked "1990 EC." Bought at a store in Volant, Pa. that specializes in musical stuff nobody really needs. For "West Wing" fans, Volant is where they shot the segment that took place in farm country and Josh, Donna, and Toby missed the tour bus and had lots of problems getting back to Washington. Since Volant is a few miles north of New Castle, just an hour or so from the Pittsburgh Airport and even less time to the Youngstown Airport, it's amazing that smart people like them had so much trouble getting back. Even more amazing was they didn't pass one Amish horse and buggy while trying.

221 *The Beatles.* 4½" tall with realistic plastic hair and movable heads. Marked "The Beatles, Lic by Seltaibing Newsent Ltd 1964," bought at the Heritage Trail Antique Mall in Wilmette, Illinois. Notice that Paul has a left-hand guitar.

225 *Italian Band.* Same as cover (first entry).

235 *Kneeling Clarinetist.* Handmade in Austria, ceramic, 6" tall and marked "Anzengruber."

241 *Bonzo Dog Horn Player.* 3" tall, bisque, marked "Studdy." He's part of a trio of Bonzos.

245 *Drummer with Wandering Eyes.* "Made in Japan," 5" tall, ceramic.

247 *Three Pink Pigs.* Ceramic, 2" tall, made in Germany. These are the musicians that started my collection. Judy had them since childhood, but her bass drummer was missing an ear. So, at every flea market, antique mall, antique store, at every yard and garage sale that we went to, I hunted for a two-eared bass drummer to replace my wife's defective pig. For years I looked, with great nonsuccess. Since I didn't want to go away empty-handed... well, you can figure out the rest. About two years ago, in an antique mall in Indiana, I found the bass drummer you see here. It's exactly the same as Judy's one-eared guy except he has holes in his head. He's part of a salt and pepper set.

Index

Abruzzi, 9
Acknowledgements, 245
Albin, Ken, 24
Aliquippa, Pennsylvania, 127
alto horn, 167
American Federation of Musicians, 175, 176
American Legion Band (New Castle, Pennsylvania), 10, 189-191, 195, 207-208, 211, 215, 230
American Legion Band (Salem, Ohio), 10, 199
American Legion convention, 199, 203
Anglos, 187-191
Appel, Mr., Mrs., 41-43
Aubrey, Janice. *See* DeVivo, Janice
Aubrey, Stu, 50
audition, 220
ax, 212

B&O Railroad, 31, 89
baby doll dance, 157
Bach, P.D.Q., 77
Band
   American Legion, New Castle, 10, 189-191, 195, 207-208, 211, 215, 230
   American Legion, Salem, 10, 199
   Blue Coat, 10, 27, 137-139, 143-145, 153, 158, 163, 184, 231
   Duke of Abruzzi, 137
   George Washington Junior High School, 119
   Highland School, 119
   Joe Dee Dixie, 3

Band (cont.)
   Mahoning School, 119
   New Castle High School, 127-129
   of America, 11
   of Anglos, 187-191
   Penn State Blue, 227, 228
   Red Coat, 10, 33, 137-139, 144, 153, 171, 184, 190, 231
   Ying Yang, 228, 231
Banda Rossa, 137
Banda Vestita D'Azzuro di Santa Margherita, 137
Bands, *Italian Wind*, 137, 167
baritone horn, 138, 190
bassoon, 7-74, 138, 171, 212, 234. *See also* bassoonist
   lessons, 69, 74, 77, 81, 85, 89, 93-94
   playing, 10, 65, 69, 97, 119, 185, 190, 216, 219-220, 237-238
bassoonist, 65, 69, 74, 77, 85, 93, 138, 219
Bassoonist, The (poem) 101-102
Beckmeyer, Harry, 190
Bersagliere, Il (Boccalare), 158
Biondi, Bebe (B.J.), 138, 139, 171, 184
Blue Coat Band, 10, 27, 137-139, 143-145, 153, 158, 163, 184, 230
Bolero, (Ravel), 10
Bonfield, Johnnie, 190
Bozell and Jacobs, 229
Brasile, Bill, 53
Bruzzese, 9
Buonpane, Tony, 116
Burnett, Leo, Advertising Agency, 231

Butcher Boy, v
button, 243-244
butt, 73

Caiazza, Bill, 243
Caiazza, Nick, 3
Calabrese, 10
Calabria, 9
Campbell, Jane, 245
Cangey, Suzy, 149
Canton, Ohio, 219
Carnival of Venice, 144
cartoons, anti-Petrillo, 176
Casbero, Anthony, 115
Casablanca, 55
Cascade Park, 12, 184
Casertan, 8-9, 149
celebration, celebrations, 27, 50, 143-145, 149-150, 158, 237, 244. *See also* feast, saints' days.
Charisse, Cyd, 244
Chautauqua Symphony, 97
Chicago, Illinois, 231-232
Chicago Lyric Opera, 109
Chicago Symphony Orchestra, 32, 109
Chicks of '56, 223
Christmas, 11, 237-238
Cincinnati Conservatory of Music, 219
clarinet, 15, 37, 212, 229-230
   lessons, 3-4, 19, 27-28, 32, 33, 42, 53-56
   music, 16
   player, players, *ix*, 15, 33, 65, 81, 138, 216, 237-238
   recitals, 11
   teacher, 3-4, 27-28, 33, 34, 53-56, 65

Clary, Kevin and Barbara, 228
Claus, Santy (Santa), 183-185
Clause, Jimmy, 183-185
Colella
   Albert, 3, 11, 15, 27-28, 33, 37, 42, 53, 65, 116, 138
   David, 139
   Helen, 27
   Jenny. *See* DeVivo
   Louie (father), 33
   Louie (son), 11, 15, 33, 138, 237
   Mary (Ruozzo), 33
   Vito, 33, 106, 115
Concertino (Weber), 16, 144, 237
Cubbertson, Harry, 3

DeAngelis, Chasey, 243
DeAngelis, Johnny, 245
Dedication, *ix*
Dee, Joe, 3
DeLillo, Roger, 243
DeMasi (family), 33-34
DeRobbio, Joe, 3
DeVivo, DeVivos
   Alphonse, 3, 15, 27, 33, 53-56, 59, 65, 179, 183, 190
   Anita, 11, 32, 116, 215-216, 227, 245
   Barbara (Zumpella), 33, 59
   Becky, 234
   Evelyn (Meine), 10, 11, 32, 49, 65, 115, 211, 215, 245
   Helen, *v*, 9, 31, 41, 59, 237, 245
   Janice (Aubrey) (Shoup), 10, 11, 33, 48-49, 119, 220, 238, 239, 244, 245
   Jenny (Colella), 11, 33, 105
   Joe (son), *v*, 32

DeVivo, DeVivos (cont.)
   Joe (grandson), 233
   Joseph (father), 9, 11, 31, 41, 55, 237, 245
   Judy, 109, 230, 233, 237, 238, 244, 245
   Kate, 233, 245
   Lizzie, 33, 41, 56
   Maria (Bencivenga), 33
   Rose (Rendulich), 33
   Stella, 55
   Tom, 11, 33, 41, 55, 56
Dingledy, Eddie, 48
DiThomas, Dante, 243
Ditka, Mike, 127
Donati music store, 55, 81
drums, drumming, 120, 134, 195, 207-208
drumsticks, 207
Duff, Johnnie, 53, 65
Duke of Abruzzi Band, 137

Eagan, Rudy (Egizzi), 3
ear-pulling, 4
1812 Overture, The (Tchaikovsky), 195
Elder, Joan, 116
electric organ, 172
Electrolux, 31
Etude, 19

Famiglia, La, 31-34
farting bedpost, 10, 138
Fazzoni family, 157
feast, feasts, 53, 143-145, 157, 244. *See also* celebration, saints' days.
Ferraro, Mike, 190, 216
Fight Song, 127-129

Figley, Judy, 41
figurines, 247
fireworks, 9, 145, 157-159, 195, 244
Fireworks March, 158
flute, 55, 90, 190, 216
Follansbee, West Virginia, 163-164
food, 149-150, 237-238
football, 127
Frabotta, Tommy, 243
French horn, 10, 32, 167, 171, 189, 211, 216
Fries, Bill, 230
Für Elise (Beethoven), 233

Gari, Ralph (Garofalo), 243
Garibaldi Club, 157, 163
Gaspare
   Ralph (father), 153, 163
   Ralph (grandson), 163
   Louis, 163
   Victor, 3, 163, 164
George Washington Junior High School Band, 119
Greenville Symphony Orchestra, 10
Gulbransen piano, 47-50
Gurneal, Madeline, 59

Hahn, Joe, 190, 211-212, 216
Haven, Jim, 69, 190, 216
Hazelcroft Avenue, 49
Heagy, Dan and Sherry, 109
Henreid, Paul, 55
Highland Avenue School, 41, 119
Hill, Johnny, 3
Hillsville (Pennsylvania), 144
hip, 211
Homer and Jethro, 23
Huff, Vic, 77, 81, 139

ice skates, 56
Idora Park, 12
Incomplete Method für die Holzblasinstrumente, 77
Iron City Beer, 11, 41, 143, 215, 230-231
Isabella, Mike, 139, 171, 190, 211
Italian-American, 8-10, 137
Italian Wind Bands, 137, 167
Iturbi, José, 234

jamming, 203-204
Johnson Bronze, 244

Keene, Willard "Stumpy," 119, 133
Kenley Players, 33
Ketchum, McLeod and Grove, 230

Lavalle, Paul, 11
Lewis, Edwin, 116
Lieutenant Kiji Suite (Prokofiev), 232
Lombardo
   Johnnie, 34
   Ralph, 34, 149, 158, 163, 245
   Stella, 34

Magic Flute (Mozart), 10, 110
Mahoning School, 119
Mahoning School Band, 119
Mahoningtown, 41, 89, 119, 137
Malatak, Mike, 245
Malley, Kent, 10, 190
Mancini, Henry, 127
Mangham, Walter, 9
Mastroddi, Lou, 54
Mathieson, Susan, 109
McCall, C.W., 230

Meine
   Curt, 32
   Evelyn. See DeVivo
   Glenn, 32, 231
   Ken (father), 10, 65, 138, 139, 189, 195, 207, 211, 215
   Ken (son), 32
   Lee, 32
Meistersinger Die (Wagner), 216
Melcer, Ray, 243
Mercer Street, 10, 41
"Midigun," 149, 231
Miller, Marsh, 3
Montgomery Avenue, 37, 244
Morgan, Thomas, 15
Music Performance Trust Fund, 175
musician's suit, 179, 239
musicians' union, 171-172

Naples, Tommy, 65, 237
Naron, Ted, 127
Natale, Mickey, 243
Natale, Tommy, 3, 243
Navarra, Bob, 228
NBC Symphony, 11
Ne-Ca-Hi, 119
New Castle (Delaware), 7
Newcastle (England), 7
New Castle (Pennsylvania), 7-12, 127, 137, 149, 157, 158, 179, 189, 244
New Castle High School, 119, 127-129
New Castle High School Band, 127-129
New Castle News, 115
New Castle Symphony Orchestra, 32, 106, 115-116
nicknames, 59-61, 183

Night Train, 53
note (musical), 19, 239
Notes (poem), 20
Number 59, 151-154
Nuovocastello, 7

oboe, x, 32, 190, 215
opera, operas, 23, 105-106, 109-111
orchestra, 10. See also Symphony Orchestra
Orlando, Fatty, 3
Our Director, 128-129

P&LE Railroad, 89
Pagano, Lou, 243
Pagliacci, I, 23
Pal-Yat-Chee, 23
Park Burlesque, 243
Parlink, Joe, 207
Paton, Mr., 119
Pecano, Dom, 243
Pecano, Roger, 116, 190, 216
peckhorn, 167
Penn State, 227-229
Penn State Blue Band, 227, 228
Penn State Orchestra, 227
Pennsylvania Railroad, 158, 244
Perrotta, Nick, 54
Petrillo, James Caesar, 171, 175-176
Philadelphia (Pennsylvania), 184, 199, 203-204, 207-208, 230
piano, 47-50, 233
   lessons, 15, 19, 233
   music, 16
   playing, 10, 15, 33, 48, 233-234, 238
   recital, x, 233
   rolls, 47-48
Pittsburgh (Pennsylvania), 7, 8, 89-90, 98, 199, 230-231, 244

Pittsburgh Junior Symphony Orchestra, 97
Pittsburgh Symphony Orchestra, 85, 97
"Poem from the 60s," 101
Poet and Peasant Overture (von Suppe), 105, 144
Polland, Mrs., 119
powder, 163-164
Prelude in D-Flat (Rachmaninoff), 16
Prescaro, Geraldine, 3
Prescaro, Mike, 3-4, 10, 27, 116
pre-wedding serenade, 11
Prima, Louie, 184, 243
Pyrotechnic Guild International, 157

quintets, woodwind, 215-216

rain catcher, 167
Ralphy. *See* Lombardo, Ralph
Rauschenberg, Dale, 207
Rauso, Mary, 59
Rauso, Vivian, 59
Red Coat Band, 10, 33, 137-139, 144, 153, 171, 184, 190, 231
Requiem (Verdi), 185
Restivo, Enzo, 3
Rienzi (Wagner), *x*
Risponda, La, 158
Rocco, Emma Scogna, 137, 167
rock and roll, 172
Rosenkavalier, Der (R. Strauss), 190
ROTC, Reserve Officer Training Corps, 227
Rozzi family, 157

Saint
St. Joseph, 32
St. Lucy's celebration (Hillsville), 144
St. Lucy's choir (New Castle), 27, 31
St. Margaret's Club, 27, 137, 143-144, 158
St. Mary's Church, 9, 31, 89
St. Vitus Church, 143
saints' days, 138, 143, 157, 244. *See also* celebration, feast.
Salem (Ohio), 244
Santa (Santy) Claus, 183-185
Saphir pianos, 233
Savannah Road, 215
Schickele, Peter, 77
Schmutzig, Willem von, 77
serenades, 11
Shenango Pottery, 9, 244
Shepp, Jack, 243
Short Story, 37
Shoup, David, 33, 55
Slaughter on Tenth Avenue, 48, 244
Sons of Columbus, 157
Sons of Italy, 138, 157
Sousa, John Philip, 144
Spiegel, Ben, 85, 89, 93-94, 97-98, 220
Stars and Stripes Forever, 157, 158, 190
Star-Spangled Banner, 128, 133-134
Steubenville (Ohio), 164
Stewart, John Carlysle, 7
stinger, 243-244
Studebaker, 37, 89, 90, 97, 106, 220, 227

"Stumpy," 119, 133
Symphony Orchestra
Chautauqua, 97
Chicago, 32, 109
Greenville, 10
NBC, 11
New Castle, 32, 106, 115-116
Penn State, 227
Pittsburgh, 85, 97
Pittsburgh Junior, 97
Yakima, 69

tailor, 163
Tanner, Chuck, 9
Thomas, Miss, 119
thunderstorm, 232
Toscanini, Arturo, 11, 185
Trillin, Calvin, 223
trombone, trombones, *ix*, 120, 190
trumpet, *ix*, *x*, 31, 175
tuba, *ix*
Turandot (Puccini), 109

uniform, uniforms, 143, 163, 227, 230
union, 171-172
Usselton, Bill, 243

Verdi's *Requiem*, 185
Vesti la Giubba (Leoncavallo), 10, 23
Vitale family, 157

Warner brothers, 9
Weinschenk's, 215
Wilde, Mark, 102
William Tell Overture (Rossini), 11, 105, 144, 190
Wilmette (Illinois), 212, 233, 234, 237

Wisler, Jim, 207
witch doctor, *v*
Woods, Virginia, 15
woodwind quintets, 215-216

Yakima Symphony
 Orchestra, 69
Ying Yang Band, 228, 231

Youngstown (Ohio), 7, 8, 12, 54,
 227, 243, 244
Youngstown College, 207, 227
Youngstown University, 207
 opera orchestra, 10

Zaccarelli, Frank, 189
Zambelli family, 157

Zollar, Alan, 190
Zona, Ralph, 243
Zumpella
 Barbara. *See* DeVivo
 Mike, 163
 Tommy, 33, 128, 139, 158

If you have any questions, suggestions, corrections or musical stories you'd like to share, or if you'd like to purchase CD's of the Red Coat Band or the Blue Coat Band, please e-mail the author at
DeVivoPress@msn.com or write to BANDS, P.O. Box 783, Wilmette, IL 60091.